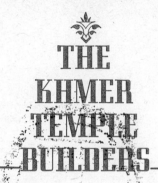

# THE KHMER TEMPLE BUILDERS

**These people, whose ancient qualities are reflected in their Cambodian heirs, are in Christopher Pym's words, "the easiest to love and the most appealing to study."**

*Pym reconstructs the lives of the Khmers from evidence found in the relics in the imposing Angkor ruins and tales like those of the thirteenth century Chinese chronicler, Chou Ta-Kouan. He describes the all-commanding kings, the priest-counselors, the world of legend where every deity had a place and the god-ruler the highest place of all. He achieves a unique and fascinating history of the vanished Khmers, from the era of the Hinduistic sacred-king religion that gave them unity, to the advent of Buddhism that altered their attitudes and brought them to passivity and acceptance of their lot as "greatness past."*

## Other MENTOR Books
## of Special Interest

By Christopher Pym

# THE
# ANCIENT
# CIVILIZATION
# OF
# ANGKOR

A MENTOR BOOK

Published by
THE NEW AMERICAN LIBRARY,
New York and Toronto
The New English Library Limited, London

Library of Congress Catalog Card Number 68-31471

Acknowledgments and Copyright Notices:
  Grateful acknowledgment is made to Presses Universitaires de
France for permission to reproduce a drawing of Angkor Wat
(Fig. 1) from *L'Asie du sud-est* by Madeleine Hallade. Quota-
tions from Chou Ta-Kouan, based on the French version by Paul
Pelliot, are published by courtesy of the Academie des Inscrip-
tions et Belles-Lettres and the Centre National de la Recherche
Scientifique (Paris). The use made of articles, drawings, and
translations of inscriptions in the publications of the École Française d'Extrême-Orient is gratefully acknowledged.

  The publishers and proprietors of the following books are
thanked for permission to quote: Osbert Sitwell, *Escape with Me*
(Macmillan); Christopher Pym (ed.), *Henri Mouhot's Diary*
(Oxford University Press); Arnold Toynbee, *East to West* (Oxford University Press).

MENTOR TRADEMARK REG. U.S. PAT. OFF. AND FOREIGN COUNTRIES
REGISTERED TRADEMARK—MARCA REGISTRADA
HECHO EN CHICAGO, U.S.A.

MENTOR BOOKS are published *in the United States* by
The New American Library, Inc.,
1301 Avenue of the Americas, New York, New York 10019,
*in Canada* by The New American Library of Canada Limited,
295 King Street East, Toronto 2, Ontario,
*in the United Kingdom* by The New English Library Limited,
Barnard's Inn, Holborn, London, E.C. 1, England

FIRST PRINTING, AUGUST, 1968

PRINTED IN THE UNITED STATES OF AMERICA

To H. M.

# CONTENTS

# List of Illustrations

## Plates

1. Angkor Wat: general view
2. Angkor Wat: bud-shaped tower
3. Angkor Wat: west gopura
4. Angkor Wat: moat
5. Angkor Wat: detail from frieze of bas-reliefs
6. Angkor Wat: from the summit of Phnom Bakheng
7. Angkor Wat: engraving of the facade
8. Angkor Wat: female figures from the upper courtyard
9. Angkor Thom: Victory Gateway
10. Angkor Thom: detail from the churning of the Sea of Milk sculptures
11. Angkor Thom: the Bayon, general view
12-14. Angkor Thom (the Bayon): heads of Lokesvara
15. Angkor Thom (the Bayon): boat, detail from the frieze of bas-reliefs
16. Angkor Thom (the Bayon): soldiers of Jayavarman VII, detail from the frieze of bas-reliefs
17. Phnom Bakheng: sandstone lion
18. Angkor Thom: terrace of elephants
19. Ta Keo: general view
20. Banteay Samre: receding pediments

## Figures

THE
ANCIENT
CIVILIZATION
OF
ANGKOR

# Introduction

Of all ancient civilizations, the Khmer is the easiest to love and the most appealing to study. An aerial view of Angkor Wat kindles the imagination, and excitement mounts as we approach Angkor Thom, the ancient capital. True, the present impinges upon us with its sentient reminders. Monkeys call to each other in the treetops. Orchids trail high above the ruins. Roots, like the feelers of some giant insect, hug the shattered masonry, and a brilliant tropical sun vainly tries to penetrate the leafy roof. From beneath rises a dank smell of decay and death. Such an atmosphere casts a glimmer of doubt over Angkor's past existence. Was it really inhabited by man? Did these bones live? Are the ruined temples an elaborate deception of our senses? There are in fact two methods of evoking the Khmer past: directly, through archaeological research, and indirectly, through a close study of their Cambodian heirs. Only by a combination of both methods can we finally see that the bones of Angkor did live, that here man constructed a great life-pattern from small beginnings and built—with a purpose—the finest temples in Asia, if not in the entire world.

The city of Angkor developed around a hill called Phnom Bakheng. During the first half of the twelfth century the temple of Angkor Wat was erected by Suryavarman II. It is surrounded first by a moat two hundred yards wide; then by an outer wall, the gates of which lead to an inner courtyard. The temple's three terraces are surmounted by five lofty towers. In the base of the central tower—most sacred of shrines—once stood a statue of the Hindu god Vishnu. Carved reliefs cover every walled surface. Some of the most remarkable, depicting scenes from the Indian epics, *Ramayana* and *Mahabharata,* appear along the lower gallery. Late in the twelfth century another king, Jayavarman VII, restored and rebuilt Angkor. The new Angkor Thom (Great City) contained an elaborate palace and, in the center of the city, another temple, called the Bayon. This temple, second in importance only to Angkor Wat, rose on the foundations of an earlier one. On its walls are many carved scenes of Khmer life—battles, ceremonial functions, work, and general forms of entertainment. Jayavarman built many other structures, some outside the city. His death marked the end of a great architectural era, for succeeding rulers only maintained what had already been built. Today, these shrines, monasteries, roads, and bridges are being recovered from the jungle after centuries of disuse.

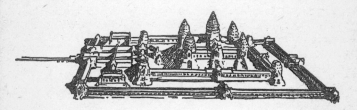

Fig. 1    Angkor Wat: general view *(Presses Universitaires de France).*

Though the ruins invite comparison with those of Central America, the Asian peninsula was never conquered by Spanish or Portuguese explorers. Spanish missionaries and adventurers visited Angkor in the sixteenth century, but provided no accounts equal to those of the Cortes and Pizarro expeditions. Their sparse travel reports were soon forgotten, and as late as 1850 the ruins of Angkor were unknown to the Western world. In the second half of the nineteenth century French colonizers took Cambodia under their protection. Their late rediscovery of the Khmers, coupled with Angkor's long abandonment before their arrival, makes this civilization seem even more remote than Egypt or Mesopotamia. Also, there has been a tendency for authors to write about Angkor, the great city, rather than about the Khmers themselves. The sole eyewitness account of this people, by the Chinese writer Chou Ta-Kouan, was recorded in the late thirteenth century, when they had already passed their height. In recent times, archaeological excavations and other scholarly efforts to reconstruct Khmer civilization have suffered from a late start and slow progress; only rarely has any stratified excavation been carried out.

What is said in this book will surely be modified by future research, and important new facts may solve some of the enigmas which puzzle us now. Yet we must admit that Angkor is today one of the world's showplaces. Like the French naturalist Mouhot, who, with the guidance of missionaries, stumbled upon the ruins a century ago, we marvel at the artistry of the temples and sculpture and try to conceive of a culture potent enough to produce them. To recall this unique civilization by examining its origins, locale, way of life, progress, and reasons for decline is the aim of this book.

# *Chapter 1*

## Origins

For six centuries the Khmers dominated Southeast Asia. Their ancestors did not spring from any particular tribe, but descended from the Mon-Khmer group, which settled in the huge area between Burma and the China Sea. Stemming from Austro-Asian origins, these tribes seem to have had a linguistic bond. In the period from 500 B.C. to A.D. 500 the pre-Khmer locale was already fixed in the southern part of that southeast Asian peninsula known today as Indochina.

The aborigines who inhabited this area met and mastered the challenges of southwest monsoons through construction that could withstand severe winds and floods. In time they discovered the benefits of river valley settlement, especially on the Mekong, their longest waterway. Generally, the tribes that lived in hilly regions did not grow and prosper, but those who occupied the river valleys or deltas flourished. There the soil was more fertile because the rivers flooded their banks annually during the rainy season and left a deposit of mud. These rivers contained fish, which the floodwaters carried into many inland creeks.

The tribal fathers of the Khmers moved from the hills

into the middle valley of the Mekong River. The flooding of this river was caused not only by the heavy rains from April to October but also by melting snow which had already swollen its upper regions. The Mekong River rises in the Himalayas on the Tibetan border, and every year millions of gallons of water pour down from the mountains. Though the Mekong was longest, other rivers—particularly the Menam—provided fertile valleys into which the tribes were tempted to move from the neighboring hillsides.

With little contact between the river valleys, the different tribes tended to develop in individual ways. The Chams in southeast Indochina and the Mons in their kingdom, Dvaravati, in the Menam River valley, are examples of other peoples who produced high civilizations; but none of these equaled that of the Khmers.

The primitive forebears of the Khmers did not look to the sea. Indeed, the word for "port" in the Cambodian language—*kompong*—refers to a village on a riverbank. No true port ever existed in Cambodia until Kompong Som, or Sihanoukville, was opened to shipping in 1955. The Khmer ancestors were not an outward-looking or imperialist people, and did not regard trade with the outside world as something to be developed. Yet though they feared the sea and were unaware of its possibilities for food and travel, they were profoundly affected by it. At the beginning of the Christian Era, the sea first brought to their shores Hindu traders from India who radically changed their way of life.

Having taken advantage of the benefits of geography by moving from hillside to river, the pre-Khmers needed the catalyst of Indian culture to achieve their highest potential. Strangely enough, this was bestowed in liberal measure on only one area of the peninsula, though more modest Hindu settlements sprang up in Champa and in those regions now known as Burma, Thailand, Malaya, Celebes, Java, and Sumatra. The ancient Khmers received important ideas from the Hinduized kings of Java and engaged in warfare with the kings of Champa, but the main infusion of Indian thought was felt most directly on the peninsula itself.

To avoid confusion, it is important to note that the name Indochina does not necessarily imply a fusion of Indian and Chinese ideas. The term was adopted in the eighteenth century to denote the surprising presence of Indian peoples in a region otherwise overrun by inhabitants of Chinese origin. Whatever affinities the pre-Khmers had with the Chinese were superficial when measured against the vast Hindu influence. Their principal contacts with the Chinese were political rather than social or cultural and were confined to diplomatic exchanges. The southward military expansion of Sinicized peoples, such as the Annamites (Vietnamese), did not become acute until after the Angkor period. We can assume, therefore, that the Hindus molded the art of the Khmers, their temple architecture, worship, and methods of cultivation. The most important influence was the Hindu religion and the Sanskrit language which embodied it.

The Hindu settlers traveled the seas in search of spices with which to trade and gold with which to make their fortunes. Their prestige grew in south Indochina, where primitive peoples, regardless of tribe, envied their status. Hindu priests, who accompanied the settlers, received invitations from tribal chieftains to teach them religious secrets most likely to bring prosperity. In return for such secrets, which included information about the technological advances the Hindus had made in draining and irrigation, the chieftains gave their daughters in marriage to the honored visitors. Intermarriage, accompanied by a significant blending of stock, led gradually to the unique Khmer civilization. The buildings of Angkor grew from the architectural tradition of Indian worship, and its art followed the iconographical patterns of Indian temples. One of the chief ideas inherited from India was the identification of the temple with Mount Meru. In Hindu mythology this mountain was said to be the navel of the earth, the city of the gods, and the dwelling place of celestial spirits. Early Khmer temples—for example, those on Phnom Krom and Phnom Bok—closely resemble Mount Meru as it is described in a work of Hindu astronomy. The Khmers, however, also developed their own ideas, which culminated in the apogee of Khmer art, Angkor Wat—recognized by some Indians today as superior to anything produced on the mainland.

Economic reasons may not have been the sole factors governing the Hindu migrations; pressures connected with caste could have contributed, too. Since the Hinduized kingdoms of Indochina did not reproduce the caste system which prevailed in India, it is tempting to link the migration from India to Southeast Asia with a reaction against the caste system. There is evidence that the Khmers traced their descent to a Hindu prince called Kaundinya, which is the name of a clan in northwest India. Settlers also came from the south, and several dynasties witnessed departures of traders to Southeast Asia. Whatever the causes, these formative waves of Hindu settlement continued during the first six centuries after Christ.

The Khmers had to be physically tough to survive, but we can assume they were attractive as well—resembling the Cambodians of today in their burnished brown skin, black, often curly, hair, and medium height (see Plate 47). Cambodian men are taller and more muscular than their neighbors in Thailand and Vietnam, while the women tend to be small and plump. Their facial structure is flat and broad, with short nose, wide mouth, and eyes which barely slant. The primitive forebears of these people were scantily dressed wanderers who chopped down trees and cleared bushes to make ricefields. They practiced human sacrifice as a form of spirit-worship to insure crop fertility. They had a spoken language, though not a written one, and buried their dead in wooden huts decorated with primitive wooden carvings. Although their rudimentary houses were built on wooden stilts and thatched with leaves, there is evidence that they knew the use of bronze and other metals for tools. Metal artifacts have been found in excavating prehistoric sites in Cambodia.

We have already established the fact that the primitive peoples of the middle and lower Mekong River valley began to be influenced by India at the beginning of the Christian era. The Angkor period dates from A.D. 802. The intervening centuries saw the rise and fall of many principalities, and one of these, known as Funan, became an important forerunner of the Khmer empire.

# Chapter 2

## Funan: Forerunner of the Khmer Empire

Imagine two concentric circles with a mutual center identified as the Hindu prince Kaundinya. So might one express the link between Funan and Khmer. According to legend, Kaundinya was their common ancestor. An Indian potentate, Kaundinya married Soma, daughter of the serpent king, or lord of the waters, and from their union sprang the first Hinduized line of Indochina, the Funan dynasty. Considering how many myths are entwined with historic fact, it seems apparent that Kaundinya's marriage denotes the great Indian migration to south Indochina at the dawn of the Christian Era, with its mingling of Hindu and Asian blood.

Skulls recovered from a Funanese settlement belong to the same type as those of primitive tribes living in central Indochina today. This places the original Funanese as a tribe of the Mon-Khmer group. They lived in the lower Mekong Valley, whereas their Khmer descendants occupied the middle Mekong region. So actually the two peoples differed only in location and degree of development. The Khmers were the avowed recipients of Funanese culture, bringing to fruition its Hinduized element.

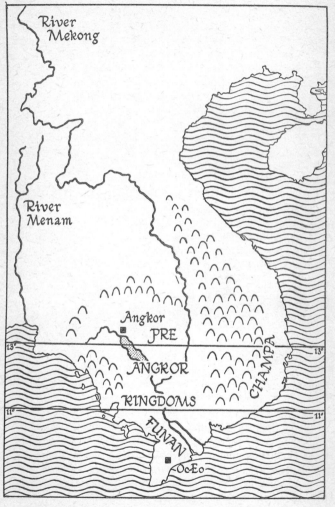

Fig. 2  The early kingdoms of Indochina *(John Stafford).*

Though never extending farther north than the eleventh parallel, the kingdom of Funan claimed and enjoyed the privileges of a great power. It maintained diplomatic ties with China and sent ambassadors to India. The history of the Liang dynasty of China mentioned "the great monarch of Funan" who built a navy and subjugated neighboring kingdoms.[1] From this and from other records we understand that the Funanese controlled the east-west maritime trade route, while furthering a type of cultural exchange with China, notably through Buddhist monks.

Chinese diplomats visiting Funan in the middle of the third century were amazed to find an impressive collection of Sanskrit books. Though natives of Funan possessed an adequate spoken language—akin to the Khmers'—they were unable to write it; hence, their adoption of the Hindu sacred tongue and Indian script, especially for religious records. It is interesting to note that neither the Funanese nor their cultural heirs ever used ideograms, proof that their linguistic debt was truly Indian rather than Chinese. Even their style of lettering may be traced to various writing systems used on the Indian mainland. These same letters were later employed to commit the Funanese vernacular to written form as a pre-Khmer language. Some examples of the Funan Sanskrit have endured, though the later, written version of their own tongue has perished.

Obviously, it was a short step from importation of a written language to acceptance of the religious life it embodied. The worship of Siva, Brahma, and Vishnu—the chief modes of Hinduism—were grafted onto Funanese beliefs. Two kinds of Buddhism were also absorbed. Worship of the Siva phallic symbols on high places and worship of Vishnuite statues in caves became general, while Mahayana Buddhism, with its many representations of the Buddha, was more widely adopted than Theravada Buddhism. Ultimately, Mahayana Buddhism resembled Hinduism more closely than it resembled any other kind of Buddhism. The people worshiped bodhisattvas as though they were incarnations of Krishna.

[1] Paul Pelliot, "Fou-Nan," *Bulletin de l'École Française d'Extrême-Orient*, III (Hanoi, Vietnam, 1903), 265.

Of all the civilizing gifts brought to the Funanese by the Hindus, the most practical proved to be an engineering feat which changed the whole course of Funanese settlement: drainage control of the mangrove swamp areas. The regions near the sea and the Mekong River delta had been impossible places for settlement or even for travel. Covered by mud and infested with crabs and crab-eating macaque monkeys, they defied all attempts of the primitive peoples to subdue them. The Hindus, by diverting sea water into canals and sealing them with dikes, conserved pools of fresh water for irrigation and even managed to supply foreign ships with drinking water. But, most importantly, proper drainage allowed new land to be cultivated with rice. Centuries later the Khmers adapted these techniques of the Funanese to the needs of the Angkor region.

Many Khmer customs can be traced to Funan. The king of Funan rode an elephant, as did the later monarchs of Angkor; both peoples indulged in pig and cock fights, and their suspected criminals faced trial by ordeal. The Funanese cast statues in bronze and built the first temples of such durable material as brick. Their homes were raised on stilts. Shaving the head became a sign of mourning, rectangular pieces of cloth were used to cover nakedness, and human sacrifice was abandoned. The Khmers did these things too. Their bronzework was marvelous. They even used brick for carving. And the practice of human sacrifice, once abandoned by Funan, was never reintroduced by the Khmers.

But the Funanese were not as architecturally sophisticated as their Khmer descendants. They scarcely knew how to handle sandstone, the chief material from which the great Khmer temples were constructed, and never carved bas-reliefs like those of Angkor Wat. In general, their society lacked the artistic sophistication and the literary values of the Khmers, who honored poets and scholars. It is true that certain localities of south Indochina yielded gold for art objects, and that glassware was produced as a trade commodity for the merchants of India and China. Primarily, the Funanese were a nation of traders and exerted their greatest influence by dominating Chinese trade routes. Discovery of Roman coins on a Fu-

nanese site indicates how far-reaching their commercial
activity was.

The place name "Angkor," derived from the Sanskrit
word *nagara* (city), appears many times in modern Cambodia, as it did in ancient times. Angkor Borei was the
capital of Funan, about 215 miles southeast of the future
Angkor of the Khmers. The site includes two hills containing caves that were treated as sacred places by Funanese
and Hindus alike. The people of Funan believed them to
be occupied by spirits. There were other capitals during
the third and fourth centuries, but Angkor Borei was the
last and the most important historically. It was there that
the Funanese and the Hindus merged. In the next two
centuries its inhabitants were not distinctly one or the
other, and the blurred identity continued until the decline
of the Funanese, before A.D. 600. Because of the gap between the twilight of Funan and the dawn of the Angkor
kingdom in the ninth century, one can erect a boundary
of sorts between them, but even such demarcation is based
more upon the lapse of time and the gestation of ideas during this interim period than upon any fundamental differences between them.

From Angkor Borei a broad canal ran southeast to Oc-
Eo, one of the emporia where the Funanese did their trading. It was, in effect, the port of Funan, though another
site for a port has been found farther south, along a canal
leading from the coast. This second canal was probably intended to protect Oc-Eo from sudden attack by foreign
warboats. Trading vessels had to obtain permission to sail
up the canal leading to Oc-Eo. There the king of Funan
allowed them to take on supplies and unload their merchandise on wooden wharves. Coral was one of the chief
materials traders brought to Oc-Eo, and in 503 the king of
Funan offered a coral Buddha to the Chinese emperor.
Oc-Eo, like Venice, used canals as thoroughfares, but
there the similarity ends. A ditch swarming with crocodiles
separated the port from an encircling mound, and the
wooden houses raised on stilts were quite rude compared
with the great Venetian palaces. But passing travelers must
have been impressed by the throng of merchants on quay-

side, the bummarees handling merchandise, and the long warboats with painted carvings.

When Oc-Eo was excavated, a square brick building (referred to by archaeologists as Edifice A) was discovered, and this presents an enigma. The absence of statues resembling those found in caves at other sites of Funan and the lack of a tiled roof and of an entrance leading from the forecourt to the central tower caused Louis Malleret, the excavator, to believe that the building might have been a tower of silence on which the Funanese exposed their dead. Certainly, black- and white-backed vultures were a common enough sight in the sky over Oc-Eo. Yet the most likely method of burial, one mentioned in the history of the Liang dynasty of China, would have been to cast the dead into the water.[2]

If Edifice A was used as a tower of silence, it provides an interesting example of a custom imported from India to Funan, but not adopted by the later Khmers. This in turn would weaken the general line of thought that the Funanese and the Khmers closely resembled each other.

Hundred Roads is another significant site that has been detected in Funan. The descriptive title of this site is of recent origin. Though not thoroughly explored, its great size (7½ by 4½ miles) and its dense network of canals indicate that it was an emporium similar to Oc-Eo. Today there is no human habitation near this site, nor did life continue on the coastal plain and in delta regions after the Funanese period. The Khmers who succeeded them would not locate in these areas, though they maintained control of the region from Angkor. This reluctance to settle near the coast can be seen even today, for the coastal strip of Cambodia is occupied by mixed populations, with a large percentage of Chinese and Vietnamese among them.

The omnipotent status of Funan's kings was made possible because their subjects linked them with Hindu gods, a belief which the rulers encouraged by associating themselves with shrines on the surrounding hills. But the religious life of the people was not sufficient to maintain this

[2] *Ibid.*, pp. 269–70.

dynasty, and a series of crises gradually brought about its decline.

After the middle of the sixth century Funanese monarchs found their authority challenged by rival kings living north of the eleventh parallel. Problems of internal security disrupted the smooth operation of the ports, and a decrease in revenue from trading made the king's position even more difficult. During its ascendancy Funan had offered safe anchorage and roomy warehouses to foreign merchant fleets, which came to rely on the fresh water and supplies they could obtain at Oc-Eo. The southeast tip of the Indochinese peninsula—Cape Camau—became a kind of Cape of Good Hope (or Cape Horn), around which these merchant vessels sailed, battling to survive. (Camões, the Portuguese epic poet, was shipwrecked there in the mid-sixteenth century and later recalled how he and the unfinished manuscript of his poem *The Lusiads* would have perished had he not been able to reach the safety of the Mekong River delta.) In fact, an agent of the Funanese king once worked as far afield as Burma, where he held merchants for ransom and threatened to close Funanese ports to their ships unless exorbitant fees were paid. This nefarious system broke down when Funan lost control of her own security.

As Funan declined in importance during the sixth century anarchy reigned in the middle and lower valley of the Mekong. The trade debacle contributed to the growth of Champa's ports on the east coast of Indochina, and eventually the Chams became a threat to Angkor itself. The last ruler of the Funan line was Rudravarman, of whom we know little except that he offered a live rhinoceros to the Chinese emperor in 539 and boasted of a miraculously long hair of Buddha in his kingdom. Funan's star had set. Fortunately, the process of Hinduizing was more than half completed. During the seventh and eighth centuries the beginnings of Khmer were evident in the middle Mekong region. Roughly 250 years passed between the downfall of the Funanese kingdom and the emergence of a cohesive empire farther north made up of Hinduized states.

# Chapter 3

◆

## Founding of the Khmer Kingdom

The pre-Khmer princes referred to the king of Funan as "Monarch of the Mountains." Their subjects in the middle Mekong Valley had witnessed the rise of Funan and had noted the importance of Hindu shrines on hills rising from the plain. The Funanese appeared to owe their prosperity to certain religious rites which these onlookers did not care to challenge. After all, the Hindu settlers had intermarried with them too. Immersion in religion was the norm, and it did not occur to them that in centuries to come its ritual would be a burden. Rigidity rather than moral purpose was a Khmer characteristic. They did not seek to build a better world; though their later move to Angkor may have been a flight from anarchic conditions in the middle and lower Mekong Valley, it did not signify a protest against their society. On the contrary, Angkor was intended to be the supreme vindication of ideas which Hinduized kingdoms had struggled with one another to master.

We have seen how Funan lost her security because of the attacks which pre-Khmer kings directed along her northern borders. The many inscriptions of these kings bear witness to this fact. Although Funan's territory did not extend north of the eleventh parallel, her predominance was recognized by Hinduized kingdoms at least as far north as the thirteenth parallel. These kingdoms, along with others farther north, took advantage of Funan's decline to assert themselves. One pre-Khmer king erected two stone statues of Nandin, the sacred ox of the Hindu deity Siva, to commemorate his victory over Funan. Another attacked Funan in 639, by which time the failing kingdom had dwindled and split into competing states, each claiming to represent Funan.

The pre-Angkor kings ruled small slices of territory, none of which ever equaled the area of modern Cambodia. The larger kingdoms covered the area of two or three provinces. In the center of such strongholds the kings built small temples which they hoped would give them the coveted title "Monarch of the Mountains." These temples took the form of several towers grouped together. Sometimes they were situated on actual hills, and the hill shrines of Funan continued to be important in this pre-Angkor period. Other centers, like Sambupura at Sambor, developed on the Mekong River itself. These kingdoms were often named after their rulers. Since there was sometimes only one town in each kingdom, situated around the sacred tower, the word *pura* (Sanskrit for "town") was simply added to the king's name; but this was not a fixed rule.

Towns bore names like Agrapura, Bhavapura, Dharmapura, and Vyadhapura. A single town might constitute a kingdom; but several communities could also be grouped together to form a kingdom. Typical kings' names were Baladitya, Bhavavarman, and Sresthavarman. (The suffix *varman*, meaning "protector," goes back to earlier Funanese times.) One or two of the pre-Angkor centers have been located—Isanapura, for example, the capital of Isanavarman I, at Sambor Prei Kuk, near Kompong Thom in central Cambodia. Vyadhapura was probably the old capital of Funan, Angkor Borei.

Some customs of this period survived through the Angkor civilization into post-Angkor Cambodia (see Plate 45). When choosing ground on which to build a house, the Cambodians still study omens. Figurines of an elephant, an ox, and a lion are made from flour and water and placed in a dish made from banana leaves. If a dog eats the ox, the land is good. If the elephant is eaten, then the prospector must look elsewhere. If the lion is devoured, the health of the future inhabitants will be bad. If none of the figurines is touched, then the land is good. Superstitions of this kind blended easily with Hinduism. Once chosen, the land could be irrigated according to Funanese techniques.

One of the pre-Angkor Khmer princes arranged for the digging of reservoirs by running a free kitchen. The name of his capital, Dharmapura (the city of virtue), indicates that the performance of such tasks as digging was a religious duty, in return for which he provided the workers with food. This was to be one of the key ideas in the Angkor civilization—the link between religious duty and the construction of reservoirs to irrigate the land from which food would come. By the sixth century the Khmers had already ceased to be primitive tribesmen, but, viewed as a whole, south Indochina was still in a state of anarchy.

Chinese travelers who visited the pre-Angkor kingdoms gave vivid accounts of the way in which a king might conduct himself. These impressions were published by Ma Touan-Lin in his mammoth ethnography of foreign peoples.[1] Every three days the king would hold a public audience. The audience chamber was divided into two parts—a raised portion like a theater stage, where the king sat amid magnificent trappings, and an auditorium, which was separated by steps from the royal crow's nest. People desiring an audience had to do obeisance by touching the ground with their foreheads three times. This kind of audience also took place at Angkor and, until recently, in Cambodia. Belief in the omnipotence of the pre-Angkor kings was scarcely concealed at such times. One inscription says that Isanavarman I was endowed with the three elements of power: personal prestige, judicious counsel, and energy.

[1] Ma Touan-Lin, *Ethnographie des peuples étrangers,* trans. by d'Hervey de Saint Denys, Paris, 1883, pp. 477–81.

Pre-Khmer statuary tells us much of this period, especially when one considers each of its three styles—Phnom Da, Sambor, and Prey Kmeng-Kompong Preah. Phnom Da is one of the hills at Angkor Borei, last capital of Funan. Therefore, this style is transitional. The earlier statues are known as Phnom Da A-style (early sixth century); the later ones, dating from the late sixth or early seventh century, are called Phnom Da B-style. The statues of Vishnu, for example, closely resemble Indian models but at the same time show a gradual shift away from the use of heavy stone block on which the statue is carved in high relief.

According to a Hindu legend, Krishna once held up a mountain which Indra tried to wash away with a cloudburst. Three statues of Krishna holding up the mountain have been discovered and are of interest because they show an identifiable bond with the art of Greece and Rome. Greek influence was felt at the dawn of Khmer art by way of Gandhara in India. Since Roman coins were found at Oc-Eo, other Roman or Greek objects, such as seals or medallions, may have found their way into Indochina. If so, Khmer sculptors working in the sixth and seventh centuries could have been influenced by Mediterranean art directly, as well as through Indian intermediaries.

One of the Phnom Da statues of Krishna holding up the mountain has a strong Mediterranean flavor (see Plate 48). This statue, known as the Wat Koh Krishna, stands five feet three inches high. It was found north of Angkor Borei under some debris covered by a nest of termites. While the general style of Phnom Da statues is usually traced back to wall sculptures in the Ellora caves of India, the Wat Koh Krishna needs to be considered apart from an Indian context, and in terms of why it seems so familiar to Western eyes.

The head of the Wat Koh Krishna is thrown upward and gazes into the sky—a feature which had already disappeared in the other two Krishna statues of this period. The statue strives to move out from its background, and the heaviness of the figure has been reduced, mainly in the damaged portions (right shoulder, chest, and right hip). This piece of sculpture most eloquently recalls classical legends about mythological heroes holding up the heavens. All of its features, especially the striving upward, the attempt to leap outward, and the heroic posture, suggest Greco-Roman models. But this work is the last to do so; later Khmer statues are more subjective. They do not gaze upward or look outward. Least of all do they reveal man.

Western eyes need a little time to become accustomed to the midnight of Khmer art. But gradually we get used to the darkness, and the shapes become acceptable as shapes in a brilliant if eerie universe. The changing details from one style to another do not illuminate the Khmers; they simply tell us that the Khmers had different ways of saying the same thing.

The apparent Western influence in the earliest statue of Khmer art illustrates another important point. Most ancient civilizations we study existed at least two thousand years ago—like Greece and Rome, which later had a renaissance. The Khmer civilization, though called ancient, is fairly recent on a Mediterranean time scale. Chaucer had been born, Notre Dame had been completed, Giotto had painted his frescoes, and Dante had died in exile, all before the ancient Khmer empire of Angkor collapsed. Yet there was no specific interchange between Angkor and Europe at the time of the Renaissance. Marco Polo did not visit the kingdom of the Khmers. It would be ludicrous, for example, to draw comparisons between what happened at Angkor and what happened concurrently in France. There may have been a glimmer of Western influence in the sixth and seventh centuries, but that was all until the sixteenth century, when some Portuguese and Spanish words were absorbed into the Cambodian language.

The Sambor style, which followed Phnom Da, takes its name from the important pre-Angkor center at Sambor Prei Kuk. Statues in this mode have longer proportions than Phnom Da statuary and their general appearance is more stylized. The few existing Sambor statues date from the first half of the seventh century. The rest of the pre-Angkor statuary, covering the remainder of the seventh and the whole of the eighth centuries, is grouped together under the Prey Kmeng-Kompong Preah style, the com-

pound name taken from two more pre-Angkor sites. There
is great diversity of detail in this long period. Male statues
have a stylized immobility about them, and female statues
are rather stiff, too. The garment worn by the female is
knotted at the navel so that it falls in the shape of a
pouch. More stone statues have survived than bronzes.
The few extant bronzes, however, already show some of
the virtuosity that was to reach full flower in later centuries (see Plate 41).

Sambor Prei Kuk itself makes a different impression on
the traveler than the later Angkor. Compared with Angkor
Wat or the Bayon, the towers of Sambor Prei Kuk seem
puny, but their submerged, ruined appearance would have
endeared them to early nineteenth-century Romantics. Ivy-
like creepers enclose the ruined towers like Balaklava helmets. One almost expects an orchestra to strike up and a
Giselle to come dancing through the forest glade. Although the forest does not seem so thick or the trees so
high as at Preah Khan of Angkor, the towers are very
much lost in the trees and sadly inaccessible. Such pre-
Angkor architecture has not been dated, but its features
are significant because they represent the heritage of the
Khmers when they became powerful at Angkor.

Besides the many small towers and cells of Sambor Prei
Kuk, which are surrounded by a rampart and moat, pre-
Angkor ruins have been discovered on hilltops—at Phnom
Bayang (near Chaudoc), Phnom Baset (near Phnom
Penh), Phnom Da (near Angkor Borei), and Phnom
Kulen (near Angkor). Although these buildings are small
in scale, they are elaborately planned, with delicate columns, recessed stories, and doorways crowned by sculptured lintels. The towers were in their own way the first
temple-mountains, the stories resembling the receding
stages of mountains. Some of the towers contained pedestals on which statues could have been placed.

Pre-Angkor ruins and objects have also been found at
Angkor itself. Their presence indicates that Angkor was
not a completely virgin site into which the Khmers suddenly moved. Archaeological remains offer evidence that
the pre-Angkor kingdoms extended over a large area, from
the old kingdom of Funan in the south to a site north of

the Dangrek hills. The remains include a cave at Wat Phu (near Paksé in Laos), which had an inscription forbidding people to clutter up the cave or to demolish its entrance, and an inscription found sixty-two miles west of Saigon. Chinese travelers were confused by the number of different kings and short-lived kingdoms which rose all over the region; but developments in sculpture and architecture do not reflect these dynastic changes except insofar as more relics have been found at the capitals of the stronger kings—Isanavarman I, for example—than elsewhere.

Although Khmer beginnings could be discerned during the seventh and eighth centuries throughout the warring kingdoms of the middle Mekong Valley, one of these must have been the cradle from which future kings of Angkor would spring. In the past it was thought that the area of Wat Phu, the site of a later Khmer temple (see Plate 32), was such a starting point, and that from as far north as the fifteenth parallel the Khmers moved south and west. But arguments for this theory were later discredited when it was discovered that Wat Phu's king was a Cham rather than a Khmer.

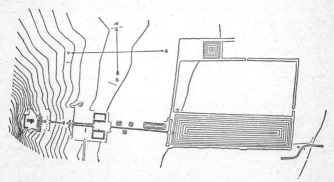

Fig. 3  Wat Phu: plan of the temple and its reservoir (*after Parmentier, EFEO*).

The breeding ground for Angkor's kings must be sought farther south, and the most likely area is that covered by the modern province of Kompong Thom, locale of the ruins of Sambor Prei Kuk. There are other pre-Angkor remains in this region, as well as prehistoric sites such as Mlu Prei, but we should not try to pinpoint the origins of Angkor's future builders in this spot exclusively. The primitive peoples who moved from hilly regions in the northwest and northeast to the river valley of the middle Mekong continued to move while the Hinduizing process was being completed. Jayavarman II, who led the move of Khmers to the Angkor region, started from Indrapura, which was probably on the Mekong River, near Kompong Cham—not in Kompong Thom province at all.

The life and times of a Roman emperor can be analyzed minutely. The same kind of dissection cannot be applied to a Khmer king or general. That Jayavarman II was an extraordinary figure may be true, but we cannot study him from enough different perspectives to put together a lifelike portrait. All books and documents of the Angkor period have perished. Ants and the hot, humid climate destroyed them. If Khmer history appears chiefly as a list of temples and kings, it is because most of the available clues are inscriptions and objects that have been found in temples. As far as we know, the Khmers did not even refer to their kings as Jayavarman VI and Jayavarman VII. Numerals have been ascribed to them for convenience because the kings of France and England are so designated. Then why should the Angkor period begin with Jayavarman II rather than with Jayavarman I? The answer is that the ruler who united the Khmer kingdom at Angkor is not the first king of that name mentioned in inscriptions. Jayavarman I is one of the many pre-Angkor kings whose capital is unknown.

Although the pre-Angkor kingdoms of south Indochina were characterized by anarchical conditions, they were not cut off from the rest of Southeast Asia. During the eighth century the Hinduized kingdom of Java exerted a powerful influence on the neighboring islands of Bali and Sumatra, as well as on the Indochinese peninsula. An Arab writer of the tenth century credited a king of Java with having made an expedition up the Mekong River and with having decapitated a Khmer ruler.[2] The kings of Java became known as "Monarchs of the Mountains," the coveted title among Hinduized princes. So it happened that while the pre-Angkor kings fought one another, they understood that the mantle of Funan now rested overseas on the shoulders of a Javanese. South Indochina was not a dependency of Java, yet its princes looked to the island for protection. An important later inscription of Sdok Kak Thom states that Jayavarman II came from Java, and women close to him are referred to several times by a term used in old Javanese and old Malay to designate a sacred person. On the basis of this evidence we can construct an account of what happened.

Jayavarman II was one of a number of petty pre-Angkor rulers who managed to establish preeminence by moving from Indrapura to Angkor. He achieved his prestige by bringing to Indochina the secrets whereby Java's kings maintained and reinforced their power. To obtain these secrets he must have visited Java and spent some time there. The mysteries that he brought back involved the important cult of the *devaraja* (god-king): installation of the god-king in transmogrified form as a *linga* (phallic emblem of Siva), placement of this linga on a temple-mountain, and initiation of the cult in each new reign. Although Jayavarman II brought these secrets from Java, they were composed of elements already familiar to the Khmers—the sacred linga, the sacred mountain, and the religious observances to be applied.

The authority of Jayavarman II did not derive from political, social, or economic achievements. He was not a road builder, nor did he expand trade or conquer his neighbors. He simply gave expression to old religious ideas and added special value to them by appearing to bring them from Java. It was as though he had said to his compatriots: "The secret of Java's kings is now my secret. I have come from Java bringing this secret with me, and once the rites have been performed my power will be im-

---

[2] George Coedès, *Les États Hindouisés d'Indochine et d'Indonésie*, rev. ed., Paris, 1964, pp. 176–77.

Fig. 4 Neak Ta
Svay Damba: a pre-
Angkor linga (Mavis
Cameron).

pregnable." He did not arrange for these rites immediately
on arrival, however. Rivalries which had divided the pre-
Angkor Khmers into tiny kingdoms had to end first; mu-
tually hostile groups had to be persuaded to throw in their
lot with him. Only then would the people abandon their
old centers, leave the fertile banks of the middle Mekong,
and join in a new life under the future devaraja.

Although the pre-Angkor period did not witness the
emergence of a stable Khmer kingdom, the two and a half
centuries that it spanned gave the Khmers time to complete their absorption of Hinduism and the chance to become a civilized people. Brick and sandstone replaced
wood as a building material. Khmer, as well as Sanskrit,
was used on inscriptions. The literary atmosphere for
which Angkor was to be noted already existed in part at

pre-Angkor courts. And Khmer social structure, with rigid upper classes of priests and kings, was defined. Khmer history, however, properly begins with the Angkor period, in A.D. 802. By that time the Khmers possessed faith and knowledge; the kings of Angkor, beginning with Jayavarman II, would crown these faculties with concrete efforts. And in such a setting the astonishing temples of Angkor would be built. After borrowing ideas from Java, Jayavarman II gently seceded from the island's influence and set himself up at Angkor. But why Angkor? That is a fascinating question in itself.

# Chapter 4

◆

# Khmer History from A.D. 802 to A.D. 1113

Various reasons have been put forth as to why the Khmers settled at Angkor. It has been suggested that Angkor was a favorable site because the region of the Great Lake was a natural center: there were sandstone quarries at Phnom Kulen; Angkor was at a junction of land routes, and at the same time was the farthest point from the sea that ships could still have access to by sailing up the Mekong River; the area was rich in natural resources; and the alluvial plain assured the inhabitants of fertile soil.

Angkor sounds like an ideal site, but none of these reasons stands up to close examination. Although the Great Lake was a natural center for the Khmers, Angkor was situated at the least desirable point in this area—in the extreme northwest. The present capital of Cambodia, Phnom Penh, is situated at a much more commanding point, where four arms of the Mekong River meet and from which the area of the Great Lake can be controlled more easily. Moreover, the sandstone quarries at Phnom Kulen were about twenty-five miles from Angkor, a most inconvenient distance from the point of view of a builder.

Although it might be argued that Angkor stood at a

juncture of land routes, these were of little importance before Angkor itself became a center, and even then they were only important insofar as they were routes to and from Angkor itself. As already stated, Jayavarman II did not build any roads or open up possible routes. The region north of Angkor was cut off by the Dangrek hills, which blocked communication effectively until the Khmers themselves built a road through them later and established their own route. Dangrek means "yoke," and the modern Thai name for these hills is "mountains of the wall." Nor did Angkor stand on the most direct route leading from the Menam River delta in the west to the Mekong River delta in the east, which would run, as it does today, south of Angkor and south of the Great Lake. The Khmers could only dominate this route by fighting battles some distance south, away from Angkor. The ancient name for this area was Malyang (general region of present-day Battambang), several times reported in Khmer history as a battlefield.

Angkor's accessibility from the sea is no more adequate an explanation of why the Khmers chose to settle there, for they were not interested in building a port. While it was possible for ships to reach Angkor by sailing up the Mekong River and across the Great Lake to the mouth of the Siemreap River, and then navigating a few miles of this small river, such an involved route did not encourage vigorous trading. Many imports were made from China, in exchange for exports from Angkor, even though the Khmer capital was remotely situated; but such was the determination of Chinese traders that these exchanges would probably have taken place if Angkor had been situated even farther inland. Certainly Jayavarman II did not have trade considerations in mind when he chose Angkor.

Natural resources such as timber and game were plentiful at Angkor, but this was also true in other areas—for example, in Kompong Thom province to the east, where the pre-Angkor peoples flourished. The best source of fish, on the other hand, was at the eastern end of the Great Lake, a long way from Angkor. The alluvial plain in the Angkor region was poorer than that bordering on the Mekong River. Moreover, it was gradually eroding. Some areas were marshy and uncultivable, and the immediate area of the Great Lake was subject to uncontrollable flooding.

Far from being a favorable site, Angkor was an unpromising place in which to found the capital of a nascent empire, and its adverse physical conditions demanded from the settlers a supreme effort merely to survive. The chief problem was how to grow enough food. The task of Jayavarman II and his successors was to stop erosion by refertilizing the alluvial plain, draining marshes where necessary and preventing the floods from coming too near. As the population increased the Khmer kings had to trap water in reservoirs and construct irrigation systems. Although the Roluos area of Angkor, for example, had been the site of a pre-Angkor kingdom, recent excavations have shown that only because of Khmer irrigation works of the ninth century were the natural forces of this region subdued. Excavations in Angkor Thom have revealed various layers of habitation, including an early layer which is sharply distinguished from succeeding layers by the absence of rice pollen. The Khmers must have brought widespread cultivation of rice to a region which had not known it.

Angkor, with all its disadvantages, presented the Khmers with their best chance of survival. Indeed, the great effort for survival under adverse conditions may have stimulated the rise of a powerful civilization. Angkor was to be the nerve center of this civilization, which did not really collapse until Angkor itself was abandoned. The rise and fall of the Khmers, therefore, is closely linked to the fortunes of Angkor. Funan, with its coastal location, had collapsed. None of the pre-Angkor kingdoms which had replaced it was able to survive; the middle valley of the Mekong River was a cemetery of such failures. By moving west to Angkor, Jayavarman II would change the course of Khmer history.

When Jayavarman II left Indrapura, he was still a small pre-Angkor dynast among other small dynasts, but he had the secret of Java's kings. He has sometimes been depicted as a kind of nomadic chieftain who camped for short periods in different parts of northwest Cambodia. This characterization of him arises because Jayavarman II's five changes of location are almost the only certain episodes in his career.

From Indrapura his first move took him to the province of Purvadisa, a little to the east of what was to become the future site of Angkor Thom. He spent some time here building up his strength before making a second move to Hariharalaya. This town, which became his capital, had already existed for one or two centuries as a pre-Angkor settlement. Roluos, the present-day village near which the ancient Hariharalaya was situated, is southeast of Angkor Thom but still in the general Angkor region. Fairly soon Jayavarman II moved again—this time to Amarendrapura, the site of which has not been determined but which probably was in the Purvadisa or Hariharalaya region. The fourth and most important transfer took him to Mount Mahendra, identified as Phnom Kulen, the group of hills to the north of Angkor from which the stones of its future temples would be quarried. Mahendraparvata, the new capital, had also been a center of pre-Angkor life before Jayavarman II arrived there.

Jayarvarman II's main achievement was to have himself consecrated according to the secrets which he had brought from Java. His reign should be thought of as having begun before this ceremony, but the year it took place, A.D. 802, is the date when a Khmer king became established in the Angkor area and when Khmer history of the Angkor period can be said to begin. The consecration ceremony had to be performed by a specially qualified high priest and had to be repeated at the accession of succeeding kings. Its effect, described earlier, was to establish the devaraja inside the linga, the phallic emblem of the Hindu deity Siva. This ceremony was performed on Jayavarman II by a high priest called Hiranyadama. Soon afterward the king abandoned Mount Mahendra (Phnom Kulen) and returned to Hariharalaya (Roluos) in the plain.

We have seen how previous kings had built temple-mountains and had vied for the title of "Monarch of the Mountains." Now Jayavarman II demonstrated that the establishment of the royal linga assured both the power of the king and the prosperity of the kingdom. Ruins of a temple-mountain have been found on Phnom Kulen (the

Mahendraparvata capital of Jayavarman II), but there is not sufficient evidence to prove that it was the exact site of the ceremony. In future reigns these temple-mountains, some of which look like pyramids, would be built on real hills, like Phnom Kulen, or in the plain. The idea of Mount Meru, the dwelling place of the gods, was the same in either case. The all-important idea of the devaraja was firmly established from this time, and it remained the driving force of the Khmer kingdom until other concepts undermined it.

Arab chroniclers of the mid-ninth century describe what must have been Jayavarman II's kingdom as a vast and powerful state where the king forbade both drinking and adultery.[1] Contrary to this description, the Angkor kingdom did not include much of Cambodia at Jayavarman II's death in 850. The achievement of his reign was the establishment of foundations on which future kings would build. The anarchy of pre-Angkor kingdoms was a thing of the past.

The next king, Jayavarman III, succeeded his father at the age of sixteen. In the year of his accession, according to an inscription, he captured a wild elephant in the forest and then lost it. A god appeared to the young king in a dream and promised that the elephant would be restored if he built a sanctuary on the spot. Two ruined brick towers, situated one and three-quarter miles northwest of the present-day Siemreap, have been discovered. Known as Prasat Chak, this temple is presumed to occupy a site on which Jayavarman III built, because the inscription about the lost elephant was found here. The inscription itself dates from the second half of the eleventh century, and its purpose seems to have been to list various donations made over the years in connection with the sanctuary. In fact, all epigraphical information about Jayavarman II and Jayavarman III comes from later inscriptions; no inscriptions dating from their reigns have survived.

Jayavarman III has become known as the elephant-loving king because of more references to elephants in the inscriptions associated with his reign. Stockades in which

[1] Manomohan Ghosh, *A History of Cambodia,* Saigon, Vietnam, 1960, p. 114.

wild elephants were kept have also been discovered. It is clear from the later bas-reliefs of Angkor Wat and elsewhere that elephants played an important part in Khmer life (see Plate 18). They are pictured carrying warriors into battle, or the king in a civil procession. Khmer elephant saddles were elaborately carved and were held in position by ropes passed forward to the elephant's collar and back under its tail. A bronze fragment, possibly of an elephant's saddle or of a palanquin, has been discovered in the Korat region of Thailand. On the reliefs of Angkor Wat a mahout is normally shown sitting in front of his master, wielding a goad in the form of a pole that terminates in a hook, probably of bronze. Elephants of Indochina have smaller ears than their African cousins, and they can be bred in captivity.

The Khmers were fond of Ganeca, the so-called elephant god. Many half-human, half-elephant statues of him have been discovered. One of Jayavarman III's successors founded two shrines in his honor, and the Hindu deity Siva's cortege included Ganeca. His name means literally "chief of the troop" (i.e., of Siva's troop), but the exact origin of his elephantlike appearance is obscure. Indian tradition holds that Ganeca was the author of an epic poem, so he is sometimes depicted as a scribe. Although the posthumous name of Jayavarman III (Vishnuloka) indicates that he was a worshiper of the Hindu deity Vishnu, he could also have worshiped Ganeca. For the ordinary Khmer peasant, Ganeca was a kind of household god. The representations of him in Khmer sculpture give him a benign rather than a horrific appearance. Madeleine Giteau, curator of the Cambodian National Museum in Phnom Penh, has written aptly that "the Khmer sculptors loved the marvelous, disliked the monstrous." Their love of Ganeca, and the way in which they depicted him, is a good example of this.

Something of Jayavarman III's character emerges in his passion for elephants, but little is really known of his reign. The devaraja cult inaugurated by his father was perpetuated at Hariharalaya (Roluos), but the location of his temple-mountain, with its royal linga, is not known. He died in 877, after consolidating the work which his father

Fig. 5 Ganeca—the god
with an elephant's head;
a favorite with the Khm-
ers *(Mavis Cameron)*.

had begun. It is about this time, late in the ninth century,
that the Khmer kingdom ceases to be known by the name
of a single town (e.g., Isanapura, capital of Isanavarman
I, or Hariharalaya) and begins to be called Kambudesa,
Kambuja, Kambupuri, and Kambujadesa, from which are
derived the present-day Cambodia, Cambodge, and Kam-
bodja. Kambu was a mythical personage from whom the
Khmers of this period claimed to be descended. *Comar* is
the rough transcription of an Arab word used to describe
the inhabitants of Kambudesa, and from it we get the

word "Khmer." (This well-accepted title "Khmer" has been challenged by some writers on the grounds that it should have occurred in written sources earlier than the ninth century.) The time was ripe for the accession of a king who would build upon the foundations laid by the two Jayavarmans. A strong king, such as Jayavarman II, would normally be succeeded by his son. If power went to some other prince—this was what happened after Jayavarman III's death—then the new king either married a girl who was related to the previous king or proved by publishing a genealogy that he was already related to his predecessor.

The new king, Indravarman I, continued to live at Hariharalaya, where he built a large reservoir (Indratataka) for irrigation and temples of various kinds. The most important of these were Preah Ko, dedicated to his ancestors in 879, and Bakong, his devaraja temple-mountain, dedicated in 881. The reservoir is dated 877 from an inscription which says dramatically that the king made a promise to begin the digging of it within five days of his accession. Both these temples and the site of the reservoir can be seen at Roluos.

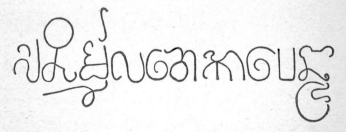

Fig. 6  Part of the inscription stating that King Indravarman dug a reservoir, Indratataka *(Mavis Cameron)*.

The name Preah Ko means literally "the temple of the sacred ox," Nandin, statues of whom were set up there in honor of Siva. Because Nandin was the sacred mount of Siva, the Khmers kept live oxen for religious ceremonies. A later inscription records how a servant of the Khmer kings led one of these animals at the head of a royal procession around the palace. Subsequently, he became herdsman to Jayavarman VI and Dharanindravarman I, and later restored some land which belonged by rights to the sacred animals but which had fallen into disuse. The herdsmen were one of the corporations which formed an integral part of Khmer society. The central shrine of Preah Ko consists of six towers, in which have been found Sivaite statues named after six of Indravarman I's relatives.

The temple of Bakong is thought to have been the location of the devaraja, partly because it is the most imposing temple on the Roluos site and also because an inscription summarizing the achievements of Indravarman I has been found there. This inscription mentions that the king founded a statue of Siva with Uma (consort of Siva) and Ganga (sister of Uma). A statue corresponding to this description has been found in an annex of the Bakong, and a second statue of three figures—apparently a replica—has also been found in the ruins. The central area of the Bakong consists of eight towers surrounding a recessed pyramid. The exact nature of Indravarman's central shrine on the top is not known, for the present bud-shaped tower dates from a later period. The inscription states that the king set up a linga here, but an excavation of the central well to a depth of sixty-six feet has not revealed anything of interest.

The reservoir of Indratataka (literally, "the sacred pool of Indra") lay north of Preah Ko, which itself lay north of the Bakong. The reservoir was rectangular and measured two and a quarter miles by half a mile. There existed in the minds of the Khmers an illogical connection between this reservoir, which provided water for irrigation, and the temples (Preah Ko and Bakong), which presided over the operation. The construction of Indratataka enabled Indravarman to feed the population, now growing fast because of the settled conditions of the ninth century. During his reign Khmer authority stretched out from Angkor over the last remaining pre-Angkor towns. Inscriptions of Indravarman I have been discovered as far afield as Ubon in Thailand and Chaudoc in southern Cambodia—a territory which formerly belonged to Funan.

Khmer history is not a recital of successive styles in architecture and sculpture, but the reign of Indravarman I marks a notable step forward in the arts. If we discount earlier reliefs on the lintels of doorways, the Bakong provides the first example of a Khmer bas-relief—a medium in which the later sculptors of Angkor Wat and the Baphuon were to triumph. Parts of a frieze have been discovered at the Bakong; a fragment shows the heads of five genies, one of whom brandishes a sword and cuts off the ensign of an enemy's standard. The composition and treatment are reminiscent of a sculptured panel executed some thousand years earlier at Cave Three of Pitalkhora in India. Both show the same muscular strength in their treatment of the figures, but there are differences of detail. The eyes of the Khmer genies are circular, whereas those of the Pitalkhora genies are oval. The mouths and broad flat noses are the same in both panels. Most of the Bakong frieze has perished, but it must have been striking in its original state.

After reigning twelve years Indravarman I died in 889, took the posthumous name of Isvaraloka—from which it is known that he was a Sivaite—and was succeeded by a son. As strong a king as Jayavarman II, he insured that his own son kept the succession. According to the important Sdok Kak Thom inscription, the new king, Yasovarman I, transferred the devaraja from Hariharalaya (Roluos) to Yasodharapura (Angkor). Although Roluos was in the general region of Angkor, this was the first time that a king of the Angkor period built his capital in the heart of what we know today as the ruins of Angkor. Angkor Thom and Angkor Wat would both be constructed in this geographical kernel. Yasovarman I established the temple-mountain of Phnom Bakheng and built the city of Yasodharapura, a locality two and a half miles square with Phnom Bakheng at the center. He also built an island temple, Lolei, in the middle of Indratataka, as well as hermitages and temples on other hills in the Angkor region (e.g., Phnom Krom and Phnom Bok) and on hills northeast of Angkor (e.g., Phnom Sandak and Preah Vihear). Besides these religious foundations, he built a new reservoir, Yasodharatataka, and changed the course of the Siemreap River so that it ran between the reservoir and the city.

Phnom Bakheng is a natural hill which the Khmers converted into a recessed pyramid. The central shrine is composed of five towers, and there are 104 smaller towers on the approaches to this summit. Although the total number of towers is 109, which when divided by four gives a total of twenty-seven for each point of the compass with one over, thirty-three towers are visible from each cardinal point. Jean Filliozat, the Indologist, when noting this fact, reports that there was an Indian tradition that thirty-three gods inhabited the sacred mountain at the middle of the universe. There was also another tradition in which the figure 109 was important—the belief in a single polar axis around which there were 108 cosmic revolutions ($1+108=109$). The figure 108 is said to be a basic number of the large year. Its importance to the Khmers is confirmed by the discovery of two pieces of sandstone at Ta Prohm of Bati (near Phnom Penh), each of which has fifty-four holes. Phnom Bakheng is the prime example of a diagram in time and space. It may also have been a funerary temple. The central tower has been excavated to a depth of seventy-nine inches, where the well comes to an end on the natural rock. A kind of sarcophagus (57 x 31 x 28 inches) has been recovered from this well, though the depradations of treasure hunters make it impossible to say when the sarcophagus was placed there. Chou Ta-Kouan mentions that the Khmer king was buried in a tower, and it may be that Phnom Bakheng was the burial place of Yasovarman I, as well as being Mount Meru.[2]

Brahminy kites, with white heads and brown backs, fly down the riverbanks and canals of Cambodia. The Siemreap River, which flows through the heart of Angkor, is the haunt of birds. Its banks are planted thickly with banana trees, betel palms, and coconuts. Today, the land on either side of the river is irrigated by undershot waterwheels, which for five miles along the banks draw up water and discharge it into fertile gardens (see Plate 59). These waterwheels, though they look primitive, are an effective

2 Chou Ta-Kouan, *Mémoires sur les coutumes du Cambodge de Tcheou Ta-Kouan,* trans. by Paul Pelliot, Paris, 1951, p. 24.

means of irrigating the neighboring land. They are, however, comparatively recent in construction. The Siemreap River did not even follow its present course in the time of Yasovarman I. The course of the river had to be diverted so that it would not interfere with the new reservoir, Yasodharatataka, which measured one mile by four and a half miles. The new course of the river flowed parallel with the north bank of Yasodharatataka and then passed south between its west bank and the city. Remains of a moat surrounding the city have been discovered, but there was apparently no stone wall protecting it. The site of the reservoir, now called the East Baray, is easily discernible though dry. Yasovarman I constructed a network of irrigation canals leading from the river to the reservoir and from the reservoir to the rice plain. Inscriptions which have been found at the corners of the East Baray praise it in extravagant terms. In the southeast corner the inscription reads, "It is by this king of kings that has been dug this reservoir with banks lined with trees in flower, raised up by means of a dike." [3] In the northeast corner Yasodharatataka is described as "beautiful as the moon, to refresh beings," and in the northwest corner as "equal to the discus of the moon." [4]

The reign of Yasovarman I followed immediately the reign of the powerful Indravarman, and the Khmers extended their territory still farther. An inscription refers to an official of Yasovarman I as the "conqueror of Champa and of other countries." After a reign of at least eleven years Yasovarman I died (c. 900), received the posthumous name of Paramasivaloka, from which it is known that he was a Sivaite, and was succeeded by a son. A hundred years had passed since Jayavarman II had himself consecrated by the high priest on Mount Mahendra. The magic of Java's kings had been successful. The Khmer king was all-powerful and his kingdom prosperous.

Two of Yasovarman I's sons, Harshavarman I and his younger brother Isanavarman II, are known to have reigned at Angkor, but the dates of their accessions and

[3] Auguste Barth and Abel Bergaigne, *Inscriptions Sanscrites du Cambodge,* Paris, 1885, p. 452.
[4] *Ibid.,* p. 502.

deaths are uncertain. It is not known where their devaraja temple was situated, but certain minor temples at Angkor, the Baksei Chamkrong and the Prasat Kravanh, are associated with this period because of their inscriptions. The Baksei Chamkrong is a recessed pyramid surmounted by a single tower. Although it has yielded no statues, it is known to have contained a statue of Siva in a later reign. The Prasat Kravanh consists of five towers, one of which has an inscription referring to the dedication of a Vishnu. Bas-reliefs of Vishnu on the inner walls confirm the Vishnuite nature of this temple. Neither Harshavarman I, who reigned perhaps until 922, nor Isanavarman II, who was still active in 925, were strong kings. The throne was usurped by their uncle.

The new king, Jayavarman IV, is thought to have been a usurper because his inscriptions, in the Koh Ker locality, date from 921, at which time his nephews were still reigning at Angkor. The inscription of Sdok Kak Thom says that he left Angkor and took the devaraja to Chok Gargyar, which has been identified as Koh Ker, a site some sixty-two miles east-northeast of Angkor. The ruins of many temples in this region bear witness to a great effort on the part of Jayavarman IV, but it is not clear just how far his authority stretched. Between Angkor and Koh Ker there is a site where Isanavarman II made a donation in 925 and where Jayavarman IV made a donation in 937. This seems to indicate that Jayavarman IV gradually extended his domain toward Angkor itself.

Like Angkor, Koh Ker was an unpromising site for a city, and Jayavarman IV was compelled to build a large reservoir, known now as Rahal, to conserve water for irrigation. A survey has revealed that there are also several minor reservoirs in the Koh Ker area. The most important building at Koh Ker was the Prasat Thom, on the west side of which stands a recessed pyramid more than twice the height of the Bakong. This was where Jayavarman IV set up the devaraja in the form of a linga and tried to repeat the magic formula of his predecessors. Remains of a pedestal (diameter 5 feet) have been discovered on the pyramid, and it seems likely that a very large linga once stood upon it. The pedestal itself, broken by treasure hunters, reveals a square chamber, below which is a deep well. Nineteen layers of laterite have been observed descending to a depth of 41 feet. Since no fragments of the vanished linga have been discovered, it may have been made of bronze or some other metal. The only bronze fragment found at Prasat Thom is a *naga* head (height 3 inches). The importance of the linga to the Khmers is confirmed by the many stone lingas which have been found in other towers at Koh Ker. For example, Prasat G has a linga 45 inches high, and Prasat H a linga 49 inches high.[5] Between these two ruins the remains of a much larger linga (height 7 feet 9 inches) have been found. The devaraja linga of Prasat Thom was much larger than any of these.

In a sense, the move of Jayavarman IV to Koh Ker was a return to pre-Angkor conditions in which powerful members of the reigning royal family formed splinter groups and set up their own kingdoms. The experiment was not successful. After reigning twenty years at Koh Ker, Jayavarman IV died in 941, received the posthumous name of Paramasivapada, from which it is known that he was a Sivaite, and was succeeded by a son. Little is known about the new king, Harshavarman II. An inscription says that he made a certain teacher president of his court in 942. His reign ended in 944, and later inscriptions give him the posthumous name of Brahmaloka, from which it is presumed that he favored the worship of Brahma. Unlike his father, he was not a strong king and failed to obtain the succession for his son. Instead, a nephew of Yasovarman I came to power.

The inscription of Sdok Kak Thom indicates that the new king, Rajendravarman II, came back from Chok Gargyar (Koh Ker) to Yasodharapura (Angkor) and brought the devaraja with him. He restored the city, built an island temple (East Mebon) to his ancestors in the center of Yasodharatataka (East Baray), and dedicated a new temple-mountain, Pré Rup. Numerous minor foundations were established at Angkor (e.g., Prasat Leak Neang) and in other parts of the Khmer kingdom (e.g., Banteay Srei,

[5] Henri Parmentier, *L'Art Khmèr classique*, Paris, 1939, p. 56 ff. Parmentier refers to these ruins by letters of the alphabet.

thirteen miles northeast of Angkor). The foundation of Prasat Pram at Koh Ker indicates that Jayavarman IV's center had not yet been completely abandoned. Besides these temples, Rajendravarman probably repaired the irrigation system of Yasovarman I, which might have fallen into disuse during the king's move to Koh Ker.

The East Mebon (952) and Pré Rup (961), though less well known than Angkor Wat or Phnom Bakheng, were achievements of which the Khmer architects could be proud. They rose like mountains from the water and the land, guaranteeing the prosperity of the empire if the worship of their gods was not neglected. The central shrine of the East Mebon consists of five towers, in one of which a circular pedestal has been found. The shape of this pedestal resembles another which has been found at a temple of the same period and which was used for a statue of Brahma. Actual fragments of a four-headed Brahma have been discovered nearby, along with a female statue. The inscription of East Mebon says that Rajendravarman founded four statues here (Siva, Siva's consort, Vishnu, and Brahma) and a linga. Perhaps the linga once occupied the central tower, and the statues, the other four towers. Below the central shrine there are eight smaller towers— probably the sites of the eight lingas also referred to in the inscription. The Khmers did not crowd into such a temple or treat it as a church. The space inside a tower where a statue would be placed was confined. Only the priests were allowed inside to perform the necessary rites. The people accepted this situation and worked to serve it.

The five towers of Pré Rup were, according to the Pré Rup inscription, occupied by a set of deities comparable to those of the East Mebon. Remains of what may be the central linga have been discovered, but evidence that Pré Rup was the devaraja temple of Rajendravarman is not conclusive. Some small pots containing pieces of calcinated bones have also been found at Pré Rup. Although these are not ancient in origin, they may explain the fact that Cambodians attribute a funerary purpose to Pré Rup. The present-day name of this temple, which means, literally, "turning the body," recalls a Cambodian funerary rite, but since the name, too, is modern, this fact does not necessarily mean that Pré Rup was originally a funerary temple.

Banteay Srei has been rhapsodically acclaimed by visitors because of its comparatively small scale—it was not a temple-mountain of the devaraja—and its pink sandstone. It must have been under construction during Rajendravarman's reign, but it was not dedicated until after his death in 968. Its central shrine, consisting of three towers, was ransacked by treasure hunters, and when the center was excavated, only a piece of rough construction stone was discovered. An inscription says that the temple was dedicated to a linga by an official of the next reign. One of the lintels of Banteay Srei shows a mountain which—as we would expect—is pictured as a recessed pyramid similar to those which had already been built at Angkor and Koh Ker. Large irrigation works have been noticed to the northeast of Banteay Srei, suggesting that it was more than a pretty little temple; it seems to have had the important function of presiding over the prosperity of the region and insuring that the land was fertile.

Rajendravarman II was a great king in the tradition of Indravarman and Yasovarman I. A Cham inscription relates that a Khmer invasion of Champa, during which the Khmers stole a statue, took place within his reign. Probably, the control which the Khmers had exerted over Champa in an earlier reign lapsed during the Koh Ker interlude. Rajendravarman II died in 968, received the posthumous name of Sivaloka, from which it is known that he was a Sivaite, and was succeeded by a son.

The next king, Jayavarman V, was related by marriage to a high priest called Divakara, who came from a region of north India identified as Mathura. Although the Hinduization of the Khmers had been completed several centuries earlier, they continued to be influenced by India and to absorb occasional new settlers. It is difficult to attribute individual monuments at Angkor in this period to a particular king. Ta Keo was possibly the devaraja temple of Jayavarman V. Its central sanctuary consists of five towers, near which various unfinished statues and a Nandin have been discovered (see Plate 19). A massive pyramid of stone, Ta Keo kneels like a giant in the Cambodian forest.

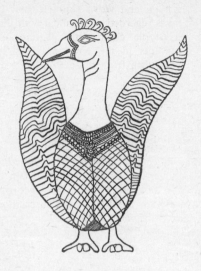

Fig. 7 B a n t e a y
Srei: a goose, detail
from a pedestal
(*Mavis Cameron*).

Although it lacks the elegance of Angkor Wat, it is stronger in appearance than almost any other Khmer temple.

Evidence from Jayavarman V's reign shows how the corporations fitted into the fabric of Khmer life. An edict dated 947 relates to the creation of two new corporations, one of which appears to have been centered near Kompong Thom and the other near Sisophon. Twenty men were chosen as the nucleus of each new corporation and were given special privileges, including exemption from certain dues. Their duties included teaching, for there were no schools as such in the ancient Khmer empire; the acquisition of learning was a religious exercise. Workers in these corporations were the Khmers' nearest equivalent to schoolmasters. They taught members of the priestly families, who would in time occupy high office. Knowledge was prized by the Khmers. There was a special Sivaite trinity which they worshiped, consisting of Siva himself, the *guru* (teacher), and *vidya* (knowledge). Each person of this trinity was regarded as identical with the other two. The common people could only acquire education by working as servants in the temples or by learning the teachings of Hinduism from those who had worked in this capacity themselves. Even though there was no conscious effort by Angkor's rulers to educate the people, learning filtered from the top of society downward. Even the smallest village had its wiseman who could talk about Mount Meru or tell stories from the Hindu epics.

The investiture of these new corporations consisted in the giving of flowers to each member and the deposition of gold- and silver-leaf copies of the edict in the court of justice. All this took place in the presence of the sacred fire, which has been identified from inscriptions and bas-reliefs. It is, for instance, carried in a procession on the bas-reliefs of Angkor Wat. The fire itself is not visible, but its container, borne aloft on poles elegantly carved with *naga*-heads, looks like a giant onion in a children's playpen. Shorn of its trimmings it looks like a linga. For the Khmers the sacred fire had life-giving qualities which transmitted themselves to those who conducted ceremonies —marriage, for example—in its presence. Although they revered the fire, they were also afraid of it. If the fire escaped from its container, it could become a destroyer. Two bronze arches, supported by lion caryatids eight inches apart at the base, and resembling the sacred fire's pen, have been found at Angkor. They suggest the existence of a cult of the sacred fire. Fire itself was a tool of the gods, and a tenth-century Khmer king spoke of himself as anxious to imitate the fire which was used in mythology by a Hindu god to burn the forest Khandava. Various inscriptions refer to a ceremony called the installation of the sacred fire. The manuscripts which laid down how these ceremonies were conducted have perished.

The thirty-three-year reign of Jayavarman V, notable for its literary atmosphere, came to an end in 1001. An inscription dated 1001 indicates that Suryavarman I was already active in the Kompong Thom region at this time.

He gradually extended his influence to Angkor, where two kings (Udayadityavarman I and Jayaviravarman) reigned in quick succession after Jayavarman V. This was another period of anarchy similar to that which preceded Jayavarman IV's rise to power at Koh Ker. When Suryavarman I finally gained control of the Khmer empire, he exacted an oath of allegiance from his supporters. A certain official called Bhupatindravallabha claimed that his twelve brothers had served a number of Khmer kings dating back to early times. His claim was not true, since it would make his eldest brother more than 200 years old. More than two centuries had passed since the reign of Jayavarman II, and impostors like Bhupatindravallabha tried to prove that they had, so to speak, "come over with the conqueror." Suryavarman I, who also started out as an impostor, had to show that he excelled in all kingly qualities. Inscriptions indicate that he was well versed in the practices of silent prayer, oblation, libation, ablution of images, and feeding of priests, as well as knowing pronunciation, prosody, grammar, lexicography, astronomy, and ritual.

Suryavarman I occupied what is known as Palace I at Angkor Thom (from 1000/1010 to about 1050) and also built the nearby temple-mountain, Phimeanakas (see Plate 50). Its central sanctuary is composed of a single tower on a recessed pyramid. A hole, six and a half feet square, has been discovered in the paving at the center. The statue or linga which once was buried here has long since disappeared. An inscription of Suryavarman I found at Preah Vihear mentions that he established a series of lingas, three of whose sites have been identified as Phnom Baset, Phnom Chisor, and Preah Vihear. The last-named temple perches like a seagull on a precipice of the Dangrek hills. Both Preah Vihear and Phnom Chisor are approached by flights of stone steps carved in the hillside. The isolated location of Preah Vihear has suggested to some writers that it was a place where Suryavarman I could retire to practice meditation and his other estimable hobbies. Traces of extensive irrigation works below the temple indicate that Preah Vihear was no exception to the general rule that Khmer temples presided over the prosperity of the land. An official of Suryavarman I, given the title of Laksmindrapandita, founded a village (Laksmindrapada) and a reservoir (Laksmindratataka), in the middle of which he placed a gold linga. The inscription giving this information, which was found at Kompong Siem near Kompong Cham, confirms that the Khmers regarded a village, a reservoir, and a linga as interdependent.

Suryavarman I was a strong king whose captains of militia included one from Louvo (Lopburi), now a province of Thailand. The Khmer empire was at this time probably quite extensive in the Menam River valley. It already occupied all the middle and lower valley of the Mekong River and exercised a dominant role in the politics of Champa farther east. After a reign of nearly half a century, Suryavarman I died in 1050 and received the posthumous name of Nirvanapada, from which it is known that he was probably a Buddhist. Doubt arises because the word Nirvana was not used exclusively in a Buddhist connection at this time. An inscription shows that Suryavarman I tolerated Sivaism and Buddhism simultaneously. This inscription, found at Pimai, contains a tribute to Siva on the front and one to Buddha on the back. Udayadityavarman II, who succeeded Suryavarman I, may well have been his son.

The Angkor region was by now covered with temples and irrigation works, but because of the growing population the new king embarked on an extensive building program. A new temple-mountain, the Baphuon, was built to house the devaraja; a new city was built round the Baphuon to replace the old Yasodharapura centered on Phnom Bakheng; and a new reservoir (the West Baray), with its island temple (the West Mebon), was probably constructed at this time, too. The new city followed the lines of Angkor Thom as it stands today, except that the walls and gateways were not added until the reign of Jayavarman VII. The king occupied Palace II of Angkor Thom, which is dated about 1050–1177. Stratified excavations carried out in 1952–1953 showed the existence of four palaces. These have been numbered I–IV. The dating of palaces I, III, and IV is problematic, as is ascertaining the *terminus a quo* of 1050 for Palace II. The *terminus ad quem* of 1177 is firmly established, since archaeological

evidence confirms what is already known—that Angkor
was sacked by the Chams in that year.

The central sanctuary of the Baphuon was composed of
a single tower rising from a recessed pyramid. An inscription says that a gold linga was established there, and a
stone linga has been discovered in the East gopura. Chou
Ta-Kouan was much impressed by the appearance of the
Baphuon, which he called the Tower of Bronze and which
he said was higher than the Bayon. The devaraja cult had
not radically altered since its establishment two and a half
centuries earlier, and an inscription refers specifically to
the king's essence residing in the golden linga of the Baphuon. The new reservoir, the West Baray, was the largest
ever built by the Khmers, measuring one and a quarter
miles by five miles. There is still water in part of it today.
On an island in the center stood the West Mebon. It consisted of a single tower rising from a recessed pyramid. A
large circular pedestal, fragments of which have been discovered, must have served as the base for a statue. The
central well of the West Mebon was excavated without result, but some bronze fragments, including a fine bronze
hand (fourteen inches long), were found nearby. Then
one of the local Cambodians had a dream in which he
claimed that Buddha had indicated to him the site of a
long-since-buried statue. This alleged revelation was instru-
mental in bringing about the discovery of a large bronze
head and other pieces of a recumbent statue (height four
feet nine inches). Water once flowed from the navel of
this statue, which has been identified as Vishnu. Such large
Khmer bronzes are extremely rare, though in the days of
Angkor there must have been many of them. The later
Thai and Annamite invaders, as well as the Cambodians
themselves, melted down statues in order to obtain the
gold and other metals from which they were made.

An inscription placed at the foot of the Baphuon records three rebellions in the reign of Udayadityavarman
II. The first of these broke out to the south of Angkor in
1051 and was put down by a Khmer general, Sangrama.
The first objective of any rebel was to sack the lingas of
his opponent's supporters, since the linga was the embodi-
ment of authority. When peace came, the losing side would

sometimes gather up the remains of broken lingas and use the stone to make new lingas. The breaking of a linga at Preah Kset, six and a quarter miles south of Chongkal, places the second rebellion some thirty-one miles north-west of Angkor. This second revolt by Kamvau, a former general of the king, and another one shortly afterward by three dissident officers, took place in 1065. Sangrama was allowed to keep the spoils of these battles because, according to the inscription, the king preferred the fidelity of his general to the spoils of war—a not uncommon occurrence in the history of empires. The Khmer empire was no exception to the way in which power may be balanced between the head of state and an influential general. Neither Kamvau nor Sangrama rose from among the common people; both men came from the priestly class.

Although the finest temples had not yet been built and the empire had not yet reached its fullest extent, the mid-eleventh century was a golden era for the Khmers. A Cham invasion was repelled and the kingdom prospered as never before. Udayadityavarman II, whose reign lasted sixteen years, died in 1066 and was succeeded by his younger brother, Harshavarman III. Ten years later the Chinese decided to attack Dai-Viet (Annam) in northeast Indochina and persuaded both Chams and Khmers to attack from the south. During the next century Khmer attacks on Dai-Viet were to become a regular feature of Khmer history. Their general ascendancy over Champa now crept gradually northward.

The death of Harshavarman III in 1080 enabled a new dynasty of kings to seize power. A later inscription says that the new king, Jayavarman VI, took control of Yasodharapura (the city currently centered on the Baphuon) but founded his capital at Mahidharapura. Since the inscriptions of Jayavarman VI and of his immediate successors predominate north of the Dangrek hills—another area which had come under Khmer domination—Mahidharapura was probably in this region. A temple was built there at Pimai, about thirty-one miles east of Korat in Thailand. Its central sanctuary consists of a square tower dedicated to the deity Vimaya. Two large statues of Vishnu, and statues of Siva with his consort, have been discovered on the site, which later, in 1108, became Buddhist. Although Jayavarman VI held sway north of the Dangrek hills, his and his successor's inscriptions have also been found in south Cambodia. The Khmer empire still held together as a unit and there was no return to pre-Angkor conditions.

We have seen how the successors to Jayavarman II built reservoirs and temples and how they made good their founder's boast that with the secret of Java's kings the power of the devaraja could be made impregnable. The temple-mountains had been built regularly and their connection with the gods of Hinduism assiduously maintained. In all this the Khmer kings were supported by the priests, who were powerful in their own right, often related by marriage to the royal family, and who worked with the kings in the building of temples and the development of land. We shall now examine how the Khmers developed their land, the challenge which the economic conditions of Angkor imposed upon them, and the great achievement of Khmer architecture, which gave meaning to their hard labors in the rice fields.

# Chapter 5

## Life in the Khmer Kingdom

### THE CHURNING LEGEND

A unique correlation of religion, economics, and art governed the ancient Khmers. Their life owed its character to one inescapable fact: a rain cycle of six months followed by a half-year of drought. Irrigation made possible the growing of rice, and rice was the mainstay of existence. Indeed, if rain could have been spread over a period of twelve months, the remarkable temples might never have been built. Fear of drought underlay many religious customs, and the erection of temples became one form of insurance for the desired end—success in the rice harvest (see Plate 46).

To this day Cambodians perform certain rites which originally were intended to produce rain. For instance, ancient stones or statues must be returned to the ground or to river bottoms where first discovered—otherwise rain will not fall. Some of these rituals have lost their religious significance and are now performed as games, but their origins seem clear enough. One game, the Sailing of the Bamboo Boats, consists of dragging pieces of bamboo over the soil and derives from an ancient custom noted by the visitor Chou Ta-Kouan in the thirteenth century.

Apart from drought, there was another natural threat to soil fertility caused by the climatic cycle: the building up of iron-oxide deposits on rocks caused by gathering water where the surface soil is not deep. Such oxidation quickly accelerates, leading to the sudden disappearance of the remaining soil. Since water can no longer penetrate the thick laterite (iron oxide) core, it rapidly removes top soil. The nourishment of the ancient rice fields lay in the alluvial chemicals of the muddy seedbed. When loss of soil deprived them of these chemicals, the result was sterility.

The problem at Angkor, then, was twofold: to irrigate the rice fields and to replace the nutritious mud which was continually being washed away. Capturing the waters of the Siemreap River in large reservoirs offered a full solution, since these river waters were muddy and furnished the much-needed chemical agents—though the greater amount of mud deposited by the Mekong River makes one wonder again why Angkor should have been chosen for the Khmer capital. To fill the reservoirs, rain had to be drawn off the hills or from the river as soon as it fell; even during the rainy season in the Cambodian region there is no prospect of rain every day. As a matter of record, the area around Angkor has only a hundred days of actual rainfall per year.

Besides the larger reservoirs at Angkor, there were sizable reservoirs and series of pools in the provinces. Some of the smaller ones had picturesque names such as Mango Basin, Buffalo Pond, Orange-Tree Pond and Brick Basin. Rice fields were also identified by name: Narrow Water, Sandy Rice Field, Broken Cart. Even the little streams were immortalized with titles: River of the Mangoes, River of the Pigs, River of the Crocodiles' Mound. Spotted rosy pelicans, gray and purple herons, white egrets with black legs, and bronze ibis frequented the shores of many of the pools and reservoirs. Lotus flourished there, and the visual effects must have been beautiful. Looking down into the water, the Khmers saw lotus buds. Looking up, they saw the bud-shaped towers of their own temples.

Although the reservoirs and pools were artificial, the bordering land sometimes provided natural banks. By taking advantage of these undulating stretches and of the natural fall of water, reservoir sites could be strategically planned to capture the maximum amount of river water at just the right time. Besides the three main reservoirs which surrounded the city of Angkor Thom on three sides, the Siemreap River was intersected by an elaborate system of canals. The network of canals inside Angkor Thom had to be linked to those outside so that a continuous flow of water through the system could be maintained. Sewers beneath the wall of Angkor Thom provided this connection. At least nine of them have been discovered. Architecturally, the sewers were a series of arches of varying heights to fit the general slope of the land. Similar arches were used for building bridges. Though most of the rice-growing area lay outside the city, there were rice fields within its walls, also, and Angkor Thom became a nerve center for the whole agricultural system.

Dikes kept water in the reservoirs or moved it along the canals and were therefore enormously important. By planning dikes cleverly, the reservoirs could be used as gravity-feed tanks, supplying water when needed to lands at lower levels. To control the level of water, the Khmers used wooden sluice gates or, possibly, heaped-up earth. Sandstone and laterite fragments have been found near a dike, and the remains of sluice gates themselves have been found at the corner of a reservoir. When the meanings of certain as yet untranslatable words in Khmer inscriptions are known, references to these sluice gates may be found.

As the Khmer population of Angkor and of the provinces expanded, the need to bring more land under cultivation increased. Their kings seem to have looked to the forest as a natural source of new land. When the king or a powerful priest granted possession of a piece of virgin forest, the recipient would uproot trees, establish a village, and dig a small reservoir. He would also build a temple. Then a new irrigation system emerged, and the area was

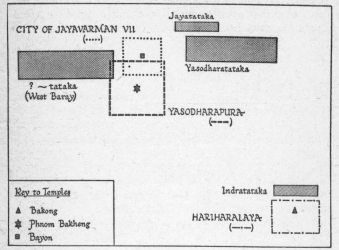

Fig. 8    Plan of reservoirs and cities on the Angkor site (*John Stafford*).

named according to the relation of its field to the main system. Such names indicated whether it was low or high land, bank rice field or dry-season rice field. Villages built in new settlements were synonymous with the land. In fact, the Sanskrit word *bhumi* (land) has passed into Cambodian as *phum* (village). The idea of living in one place and commuting to work in another was foreign to the Khmers. To them the village was intended for the land and the land for the village.

The Cambodians have some two hundred ways of describing rice of various kinds and at different stages of growth and preparation. Excavations on the palace site of Angkor Thom have produced pollen examples identified as *oryza sativa,* the type of rice normally sown in flooded rice fields. Chou Ta-Kouan also mentions a form of rice which seems to grow higher and higher as the level of the water rises. This could be "floating rice" (*oryza fluitans*), but more likely it is a rare type of rice called *srangne* by present-day Cambodians. This species, found in the Battambang region of Cambodia, grows to such a height that it must be harvested by boat. *Oryza sativa* is not harvested until the water has drained from the field.

Fig. 9   Khmer farmers planting rice *(Mavis Cameron)*.

The Khmer farmer prepared his ground with a plow-share pulled by oxen or water buffalo. One of the battle scenes of the Angkor Wat bas-reliefs shows a plow brandished as a weapon. This sculptured plow is almost identical with the kind used in rural Cambodia today. When the land had been plowed and watered, the Khmers took bunches of rice seedlings grown in nursery fields and planted them. This was backbreaking work. An inscription refers to the need for keeping water buffalo under control and preventing them from trampling on designated areas of temple property—a rice-growing area perhaps. During the rainy season the buffalo were brought into the village and rubbed down at night to keep them from catching cold. In the dry season they would be allowed to graze several miles from habitation.

Fig. 10 Plowing—an activity of the farmer-builder-soldier class (*Mavis Cameron*).

Marauding animals often menaced the rice ready for harvest. An inscription records that a royal official killed two elephants who ate his growing crops; later he had to give a piece of land to their owner to compensate him for the loss of his animals. After the crops were harvested with sickles, the rice was carried in oxcarts to the village and stored in rooms of domestic houses set aside for this purpose. Part of the crop had to be given to the king and part to the local temple. There were large granaries at Angkor where the king stored his rice, and a special officer had charge of the cereal stocks. In time the chaff was separated from the grain; a bas-relief of Banteay Chhmar shows victims in hell pounded in a rice mortar similar to those now used in Cambodia for removing husks. The chief gap in our knowledge of Khmer rice production is the absence of any statistics. Chou Ta-Kouan says that there were three or four rice harvests every year.

At least two, possibly three, of these harvests were attributable to the large water supplies at Angkor and to the systematic way they were used to irrigate the land during the dry season. The irrigation system made it possible to provide the thousands of tons of rice needed for a growing population.

Fig. 11   Khmer farmers harvesting rice *(Mavis Cameron).*

A typical survey of rice-bearing land mentions that a certain property was bordered on the east by a clump of tamarisks, on the south by the foot of a hill, on the west by a pool, and on the north by a river. When no natural borders existed, border stones were put down. Removing them was strictly forbidden. These stones had descriptive names like Marsh of the Leeches Stone; boundary locales also had titles, such as Hillock of the Myrobolan Tree or Runaway Hare Region. One boundary stone bore the following inscription: "This is the land of the lord Rajahputra of the port of the Coconut Palms." Wooden boundary posts were also used, one of which has been discovered at Preah Ko. Units of land measurement varied. Sometimes fields were given numbers; for example, "lands to the number of eight," meaning that eight plots of land made up one intensively cultivated property. Such land division prevented waste. After Angkor fell, the Cambodians returned to the custom of cultivating large plots, wasting land at the corners where their plows turned. Ancient Khmer fields were sometimes measured by "scatterings of grain" or by "baskets" of grain.

Neither king nor priests owned all the lands in the kingdom. Even the portion owned by the temples was comparatively small—perhaps a sixth of the whole. Most of the land was owned by the farmer-builder-soldier class, but the heavy donations of rice these people owed the temples and the ruler turned them into serfs. The amount of rice which they had to contribute is uncertain, but they doubtless gave more than a tithe. Assessments were made by a member of the royal public service. Owners were then informed of the amount of produce to be surrendered at harvest. Would-be evaders sometimes claimed that their rice fields had a higher output than had officially been assessed. One would expect them to have claimed that their output was lower, for this would have reduced the amount of tax. However, they had their reasons. Certain rice fields in each village had to surrender their total output to the temple. If farmers were caught withholding produce from such fields, they were taken to court. Their only defense was to claim that the output was higher than had officially been assessed, and that they had merely kept the difference between estimated and actual figures.

Land in the ancient Khmer kingdom frequently changed hands; indeed, one official at Angkor acted as guardian of the sealed acts of property. Rice field transactions were complicated by the fact that the Khmers had no coinage. The price of a rice field might be ten water buffalo, and more extensive lands would be reckoned in terms of gold, silver, cloth, or slaves. Although ownership might change, obligations to king and temples remained constant. When property was transferred, it was customary to check boundaries so that there would be no dispute later. If land had been bought for a temple, there might be a special ceremony at which a clod of earth was offered in each of the temple's storehouses. One inscription specifies how the rice fields of a small temple were to be managed—those southeast of the pool by two cooks, and those in other directions by two makers of leaves (for writing), by musicians, and by dancers.

Maintenance of their temples placed an ever-increasing burden on the Khmers. When a new temple was built at Angkor, villages from remote districts had to contribute, even if they were already contributing to other temples, both locally and in Angkor, too. But though reluctant at times to meet their financial obligations, the Khmers had an overwhelming sense of commitment. After all, the great theme of Khmer architecture promised an end to their fatigues in some future life and increasing affluence in this one. Everything harked back to the legend of the churning of the Sea of Milk, which gave hope and meaning to each toiling peasant.

The legend is well known in India, where it finds expression in a painting of the Mahakali temple at Chanda (Madhya Pradesh). It also appears as a tiny decorative motif on a Chandella Vishnu in the British Museum and on a lintel of Cave III of Badami (Bijapur). Examples in Khmer sculpture and architecture include an avenue of figures outside the five gates of Angkor Thom, similar ones outside Preah Khan of Angkor, and the bas-reliefs of Gallery D. in Angkor Wat. Provincial representations also abound.

When Chou Ta-Kouan approached the gateways of Angkor Thom, he described them as follows:

> Outside the wall is a large moat; outside the moat there are large bridges with roads coming in. On each side of the bridges, [there are] fifty-four stone divinities which have the appearance of "stone generals"; they are gigantic and terrible [see Plate 10]. The five gates are similar. The parapets of the bridges are entirely carved in stone, in the form of serpents which

all have nine heads. The fifty-four divinities all hang
onto the serpent with their hands and look as though
they are trying to stop his running away.[1]

Chou Ta-Kouan's "stone generals" can be seen at Angkor today. They look as if they are engaged in a tug-of-
war. During the celebration of the Cambodian New Year,
girls and boys take part in a tug-of-war which stems from
the churning legend and which is intended to produce
heavy rainfall in coming months.

Derived from Hinduism, the churning legend unfolds as
a continuing action. Vishnu, in his incarnation as Kurma
the tortoise, sits himself on the ocean bed of the Sea of
Milk and offers his shell as the base for the mountain
Mandara. This mountain acts as a stirring instrument,
which, when rotated, will stir and churn the sea below. In
order to set the mountain in motion, the gods and demons
—Chou Ta-Kouan's "stone generals"—twist a serpent's
body around it. Then, by pulling the serpent backward
and forward, they churn the water. The purpose of this
operation is to recover important lost objects. If the churning movement is performed successfully, the lost objects
are thrown up out of the sea and recovered. In Hindu mythology, where this legend is often told, ambrosia—the
source of immortality—is one such important lost object.
Others include the cow of plenty, the goddess of good
fortune, and the nymph of loveliness. An inscription
describes one of the rewards for perseverance in churning as "putting to an end the sufferings of fatigue." This
much-desired reward and the legend itself are closely
linked with the digging of a pool—for irrigation purposes.

Ambrosia and other objects recovered by churning must
be equated with prosperity. For most of the Khmer people
this meant adequate food rather than riches. Prosperity
depended on a harvest of more than one crop annually, a
feat made possible by the irrigation systems. The idea of
obtaining ambrosia was an ancient one: a Funanese inscription refers to an area transformed into a lake of the

[1] Chou Ta-Kouan, p. 10.

Fig. 12   The churning of the Sea of Milk, detail *(Mavis Cameron)*.

treasured substance. The temples and reservoirs were interdependent. Khmer kings could not construct reservoirs for purely economic reasons. They were compelled to clothe this operation in religious guise by building a temple at the same time. Obviously, the social activity of irrigating rice fields could not be effective unless the whole irrigation system was hallowed as part of a monument built for, and offered to, a god.

It is absurd to say that the East, West, and North Barays at Angkor existed to provide washing or drinking water. It is only a little less absurd to suggest that they existed primarily for ceremonial bathing, although such bathing is known to have taken place. Enormous expanses of water like these reservoirs, viewed objectively, must have been established for one purpose only—to irrigate the land. As we have seen, water from any of these three reservoirs could be conducted by canals to the moat of Angkor Thom and then expelled. Water in the moat flowed under the bridges where Chou Ta-Kouan's "stone generals" performed their churning operations. The result of this churning—prosperity—was thus most clearly carried by the same water; eventually it reached the parched rice fields, and transformed them into an ocean of ambrosia. The building of temple-mountains and the cult of the devaraja were also indispensable parts of the scheme. The connection between a temple-mountain and the provision of water has survived to the present day. Cambodians, especially in the Angkor region, make pyramidal sand castles at New Year's time and sprinkle water on them to induce rain. The economy, religion, and art of the Khmers are indivisible; the churning legend of Hindu mythology provides the link between them.

## THE SOCIAL ORDER

The Khmers may have longed for riches, but only in a collective sense. The prosperity of the kingdom mattered more than individual wealth. Each class had its appointed role, just as the towers of Angkor Wat had a definite meaning in Khmer cosmogony. The king built a temple and the peasant built a house according to a set of rules. If the rules were broken, the magic relationship of temples or houses to the land would be broken. Other bonds—such as those of the common people with the land, the common people with the king, and the king with the gods—would be weakened as well.

When a Cambodian house is consecrated, a pregnant cat takes part in the procession around the new property. This animal represents Lakshmi, the Hindu goddess of plenty and one of the longed-for objects produced by the churning of the Sea of Milk. The cat in her pregnant state is a token of fertility, without which there can be no plenty. According to Cambodian legend, the first female cat came from the menstruation of a woman. If a pregnant cat jumped over a corpse, the departed spirit returned momentarily to the body. Though the rules for consecrating houses at Angkor have been lost, we can reconstruct them through legend and modern custom. The house of a Khmer peasant was a link in the magic chain of events leading toward prosperity. Peasants built temples and farmed the land; these acts were the keys to a rich Khmer kingdom.

Khmer society was neither classless nor democratic. The ruling classes were hereditary kings and priests. But a king might be overthrown, just as in our own day rulers of small states are dislodged in palace revolutions. The palace revolution was common at Angkor. Power could be wrested away by a rival, but only if he acted according to the accepted code of rules. For instance, a usurper could not hope to maintain his position unless he could prove his blood relationship with a previous king. At Angkor it was normal for a king to trace his ancestry back to Jayavarman II, with whose reign the Angkor period in Khmer history begins (A.D. 802). The all-powerful kings were regarded as gods by their subjects and were worshiped in their own lifetimes. But they were also considered super beings in a human sense and were reputed to excel in all skills. It was said of Yasovarman I, for example, that in the exercise of wrestling he lifted ten wrestlers in a moment and hurled them onto the ground in a heap. So powerful were the superhuman Khmer kings that they could make their subjects serve, obey, and, if need be, die.

Below the king, the most important section of the Khmer population was the great family of priests. In real-

ity, there were many families of priests, but each family
tried to trace its ancestry back through the female line to
the priests who had served Jayavarman II. The most important priest was the *purohita* (high priest), then came
the *hotar* (royal chaplain) and the *upadhyaya* (royal pre-
ceptor). Other *hotars* (chaplains) and *gurus* (teachers)
held less important posts in the king's entourage. As more
temples were built in the Angkor region the number of
priests increased. Sacrificers and curators were added to
the hereditary appointments. Among the minor priests
were scholars, poets, astrologers, and doctors of metaphys-
ics. After three hundred years of Khmer rule at Angkor
there were so many persons eligible by birth for priestly
office that the hereditary appointments system broke down
and the Khmer kings simply appointed priests of their
own choice to the various jobs. But the power of the
priests was in no way lessened. This great family owed allegiance to the king and effectively prevented the rise to
power, either as priest or monarch, of anyone from the
common people. Since they enforced the rules, the priests
were indispensable to the Khmer kingdom's prosperity.
Without them the system could not work.

Below the king and the priests came the corporations,
organized according to trade. This division of people by
trade (gem cutters, herdsmen, etc.) and the fixing of their
social position by the relative importance of their work recalls the caste system of India. But there is no conclusive
evidence that castes in the full Indian sense existed at
Angkor, and so we must confine ourselves to speaking of
"corporations"—a suitably vague term. A family might
serve the Khmer king in a particular capacity—as bronzeworkers, for example—but there was some relaxation of
the system, whereby persons could pass from another corporation into that of the bronzeworkers. Members of these
corporations were an important link in the chain of a
Khmer's destiny. Wrestling in one of the king's entertainments, for instance, was a religious duty for members of
the wrestling corporation. If this duty was not performed
at the proper time in the correct way, it was believed that
the future well-being of the kingdom would be impaired.

Complicated sets of rules bound the corporation members into the fabric of Khmer life.

The next important level of Khmer society was comprised of the captains of militia. Though the king, who led his country into battle, sometimes engaged his chief enemy in single combat, Khmer military strength rested on the junior officers, the captains of militia. These men commanded the loyalty of peasant groups in their particular locality. If the king conquered a region, a new captain of militia would be enrolled and put under an oath of allegiance. The captains were simply headmen of the outlying regions, but their connection with the king enhanced their status. In time of war they were expected to conscript the peasants in their district and to lead them to Angkor to join the Khmer army. If the captains disobeyed the king, they were put to death.

The vast majority of the Khmer population were of the farmer-builder-soldier class. They cultivated the land to produce the vital rice on which Khmer economy depended. They built the great temples whose ruins now stand in the forest as silent witnesses to their service. They fought the king's battles in time of war. The whole structure of Khmer society was designed to keep these men at work—though not consciously so. They planted, built, and fought because it would never have entered their minds to do anything different—at least not during the Angkor period of Khmer history.

These farmer-builder-soldiers had no liberty, nor did they think in terms of liberty or know that they lacked it. They were serfs, tied to the soil they plowed, to the temples they served, and to the king's army, in which they were obliged to fight. The full burden of Angkor's destiny fell on those who made up this section of the community, but they had no means of modifying that destiny or of exerting controls. They could only serve their ultimate masters, the priests and the king. There was a crude logic to their philosophy of life. The land needed temples; the temples needed the land. As they bent their backs planting rice or hauling blocks of sandstone up to great heights by pulley they were unable to see that the two operations were not related. For the Khmers, every moment of their lives was part of a well-regulated pattern. When they heard the gong strike each hour of the night from a tower of Angkor Thom, it served to remind them of this pattern. The temples, which were inexorable diagrams of time and space, reflected the pattern.

There remains only one more level of Khmer society to consider—the slaves. Made up of debtors, prisoners of war, and tribesmen from the hilly regions, it was probably the slave class that performed the roughest tasks of all— working the quarries, rowing the warboats, and dredging the irrigation canals. Like the Roman slaves, they could obtain their freedom. An inscription states: "By favor of the king toward this man [not named], Prabhasoma, wife of Somati, has obtained liberty with her sons and her grandsons." Despite the fact that those at the bottom of Angkor's society might better themselves, the Khmers generally remained in that stratum of society into which they were born. The dividing line between the farmer-builder-soldier class and the slaves is hard to discern, though Chou Ta-Kouan says emphatically that everyone at Angkor owned slaves except the very poor. The poor could be reduced to slavery if they fell into debt. But the two chief sources for slaves, as already mentioned, were war prisoners and hill tribesmen.

Prisoners helped build the great temples, but they did not constitute the major part of the building force. The inscription of Preah Khan (Angkor) mentions four nationalities of slaves working at that time: the Campa (Chams), the Pukam (inhabitants of Pagan), the Yavana (Annamites), and the Rvan (Mon, or inhabitants of Pegu). These slaves must have been captured in war. A bas-relief of Angkor Wat shows a contingent of Thais in the Khmer army, but they were possibly allies rather than slaves at that time. In the thirteenth and fourteenth centuries, when the Khmers and Thais fought each other, each side would have enslaved the opponent's soldiers.

The Khmers, themselves descended from a tribal nucleus, despised the various tribes who lived in the hills of Indochina and had missed being influenced by Hindu civilization. These tribesmen formed part of the slave population. In one inscription the slaves are referred to as *vrau*, which seems to be the same as *brau*, the name of a mountain tribe which still exists in central Indochina today. Chou Ta-Kouan wrote that there were two kinds of tribesmen, those who understood Khmer and those who did not. The same is true today. Certain tribes living near Angkor not only understand the Cambodian language but have also given their names to ancient Khmer sites. One of these is Samré, after which the temple of Banteay Samré is named. Other tribesmen who lived near Angkor worked the iron mines at Phnom Dek. Until recently the Cambodian king received an annual tribute of metal from them, and even now they are not wholly integrated into the Cambodian population.

Slaves are designated in various ways on the inscriptions —for example, *va* or *si* for male slaves of different epochs, and *ku* or *tai* for females. Children are referred to as *kon* (child) or are given an additional designation such as *pau* (unweaned) or *rat* (toddlers). Groups of slaves were known either by the locality of their origin (for example, "the group from the River of the Cranes"), by their distinctive qualities (such as a *ku* "born for loving" and a *va* "who tells not all"), or by their jobs (as a cook or a maker of leaves for writing). Many different jobs besides quarrying, dredging, and rowing were performed by slaves. At a Vishnuite hermitage there were two scribes, two guardians of the royal bedchamber, two librarians, two providers of betel, two carriers of water, six makers of leaves (for writing), four mat carriers, an unspecified number of vegetable collectors, two supervisors of these persons, eight cooks, and twelve kitchen orderlies. These slaves had less onerous jobs than those who worked in the quarries, but they did not own land and were worse off than the farmer-builder-soldier class. A foundation stone mentions overseer, shop attendant, constable, farmhand, cook, musician, and flower collector as functions for male slaves; and maker of leaves (for writing), musician, herdswoman, gardener, and dancer as functions for female slaves.

Varying prices were paid for slaves. According to Chou

Ta-Kouan, a young slave could be bought for a hundred bands of fabric (one rectangular band was enough to clothe one person—see below) and an old slave for thirty or forty bands. An inscription mentions slaves bought for twenty measures of paddy or for a heifer and ten measures of paddy. Other inscriptions mention a wide variety of objects that were bartered when slaves changed hands. The runaway slave was not uncommon. On one inscription the slaves' names are extremely roughhewn, as though the lapidary, perhaps a slave himself, had intended that they be difficult to read and the runaways hard to trace. There were various punishments for recaptured slaves. Chou Ta-Kouan says that their faces were marked with blue or that iron stocks were put around their necks, arms, and legs. One inscription tells of a slave whose ears and nose were cut off as a punishment for running away.

Societies that use slaves incur universal opprobrium now, but this kind of disapproval did not exist at Angkor. The system was not one in which a few persons lived off the labor of an enormous number of slaves. If there was an overexploited group in the society, it was the farmer-builder-soldier class. The slaves were accepted as a natural part of the pattern. Prisoners of war worked mainly at Angkor itself. The tribesmen could, by retreating into the hills, escape servitude altogether. There were few slaves in provincial centers. The Khmer civilization rested not on slaves but on the Khmer peasants. We have seen already how they worked for the devaraja and for the priests and how their religion and economy were intertwined.

It is depressing, perhaps, to find that a society which denied the expression of liberty flourished and produced great works of art. But the idea that an artist should be free to express his own individuality and the notion that art should be encouraged for its own sake were foreign to the Khmers. In all their art, whether sculpture or architecture, the object was to serve a great religious ideal based on the divine nature of kings and on the magical relationship of land and temples. Because all art was subordinated to this end, Khmer craftsmen did not regard sculpture and architecture as two different arts. Both the man who carved a statue and the man who designed the chapel into which that statue would be placed contributed to the same ideal. There were no sightseers who came to admire the statue and no tourists who criticized the chapel's aesthetic qualities. Though they have become showpieces in our time, to the Khmers the temples just served their religion.

## RELIGION AND DEVARAJA

Although the upper strata of Khmer society contained highly educated persons, intellectuals as we know them did not exist. The Khmers held learned discussions, but there was a crucial difference between their debates and a Socratic dialogue, for instance. The Khmers could not be called seekers after truth, for in their own estimation they already possessed it. If they discussed the tenets of their religion, the purpose was to practice virtue, not to find answers. Talking about the teachings of Buddha or of Vishnuism was a religious act, like lighting a temple candle.

Although the doctrines of Hinduism demanded a lifetime of study, even from the Khmer priests themselves, the basic ideas penetrated downward through society and permeated the daily life of the people. The most characteristic of these ideas were the lack of free will and the prospect of reincarnation. The Khmer sculptor who molded the sandstone with loving care did so in the knowledge that previous acts in another life had won him this privilege. The fatalistic feeling that he had no control over these previous acts and therefore could not change his destiny was tempered by a hope born of instinct that things might be better in his next life. If he had no free will, he at least had the urge to go forward and liberate himself by achievement. So although the Khmers saw their past, present, and future controlled by fate, they were continually breaking the bonds of fatalism. In this way their civilization kept moving forward—at least for as long as its central ideas were kept intact.

Hinduism, one of the keystones of Khmer civilization, was derived from the Vedas, the sacred books of India. These date back a thousand years or more before Hindu settlers came to Indochina. The idea that there existed a life-giving juice, ambrosia, can be traced back to the Vedas. Legends like that of the churning passed from the Vedas into later Hindu literature, from which the Khmers received and developed them. Hindu society was rigidly organized into castes, each of which had its duty to perform. While the different classes of Khmer society also had their duties to fulfill, their system was not so rigid. When an idea or a religious belief was transported from India to Indochina, there was a tendency for it to become less exclusive of other beliefs. This enabled the Khmers to import the cults of many different Hindu deities.

Brahma, the chief god of the Hindu trinity (Brahma, Siva, and Vishnu), was in Khmer religion and art its least important member and usually worshiped only with other members of the trinity. Certain temples on hills at Angkor (Phnom Krom and Phnom Bok, for example) have three central towers, once occupied by statues of the Hindu trinity. Brahma occupied the south tower on these sites. The rare statues of Brahma show that he was usually depicted with four faces and four arms. In theory, Brahma created all things, but the Khmers attributed creation to Vishnu and Siva.

Vishnu, the second god of the Hindu trinity, is usually represented in Khmer art with four arms holding four objects: discus (upper right hand), ball (lower right hand), conch (upper left hand), and club (lower left hand). These attributes are the same as those held by Indian statues of Vishnu, except that for the ball they used a lotus. Vishnu was regarded as the creator and preserver of the world (see Plates 26 and 38). In his incarnation as Kurma the tortoise he played an important role in the churning legend, itself a tale of creation—the recovered objects being the things created. The Khmers regarded the tortoise as an animal which would bring them good luck. Gold-leaf tortoise charms have been found in excavations, and a stone tortoise was found at the North Kleang of Angkor. The Cambodians believe that the tortoise's shell and entrails have curative properties; a paste made of these ingredients is supposed to be good for applying to sprains. When they depicted Kurma in sculpture, the Khmers showed a touch of imagination. A Kurma tortoise on the wall of a corner pavilion of Angkor Wat, for instance, has a floral-patterned shell.

Another of Vishnu's incarnations, Rama, was extremely popular with the Khmers. They learned the saga of Rama, which is Homeric in quality, from the *Ramayana,* a well-loved Hindu epic poem. This was the Khmers' *Odyssey* and *Iliad* rolled into one, and was longer than both Greek epics put together. Other Hindu epic poems pleased the Khmers, but none more than the *Ramayana.* One of the most popular scenes was the siege of Lanka (Ceylon), in which Rama, aided by his brother Lakshman and an army of monkeys, sets out to free the Princess Sita, who has been kidnapped by the demon-king Ravana. This episode found its highest expression in the bas-reliefs of Angkor Wat. The monkeys and demons grapple together, tearing at each other, plunging their feet into an opponent's mouth, and diving under the wheels of chariots. Rama is the victor in this contest. Whenever the Khmers paid homage to Rama, they thought of him as synonymous with Vishnu. To worship Rama was to worship Vishnu.

Krishna, another incarnation of Vishnu which the Khmers liked to depict in sculpture, was said to have delivered the famous *Bhagavad-Gita.* The scene in Krishna's saga which commended itself most to the Khmers was that in which he held up the mountain Govardhana. According to the Hindu legend, Krishna persuaded the local people to worship this mountain instead of Indra. It became necessary for Krishna to hold up the mountain when Indra tried to wash it away in a cloudburst. Shepherds with their flocks sought his protection. On the reliefs of Angkor Wat these animals are depicted in many different attitudes. One points its nostrils upward in fright. Another looks back at the shepherds, who are trying to reassure it. The battles of

Krishna, told in the *Mahabharata,* another popular epic poem, are also depicted in Khmer sculpture. Worship of Krishna, like that of Rama, was worship of Vishnu.

The traditional mount of Vishnu was Garuda, a mythical beast half-bird and half-human. He is one of the figures most frequently represented in Khmer sculpture (see Plate 37). Garuda also carries the human incarnations of Vishnu, such as Krishna, into battle. Traditionally, Garuda was regarded as the enemy of the serpent, and Khmer sculpture repeatedly depicts him with his adversary. The idea of a contest between the two disappeared, however, for the Khmers had equal respect for the serpent, who was lord of the waters, and for Vishnu's mount. Small portraits of Garuda and the *naga* (serpent) appear on bronze fragments of Khmer furniture. A high sandstone Garuda forms part of the wall at the northeast corner of the outer enclosure of Preah Khan (Angkor). The Khmers found Garuda a comforting deity. His eagle's beak promised protection, and his wings, outstretched like those of a benevolent archangel, gave them a feeling of security. His feathers looked like the stitching on an old woman's shawl. The creature who protected Vishnu protected Vishnu's people. Garuda appears standing on plinths, as a terminal motif on balustrades (with the *naga*), on lintels, and frequently on the bas-reliefs. To the ordinary Khmer peasant, Garuda was a kind of household god, like Ganeca, the elephant-human.

Although Vishnu occupied an important place in the Khmer pantheon, Siva was for them the most important member of the Hindu trinity. The Khmers regarded him as a benevolent deity, another creator, and not the fierce and cruel destroyer of life as he is known in India. Siva was not synonymous with fear. Often depicted carrying a trident and clothed in a tiger skin, he can be identified by the third eye in the middle of his forehead. Despite his eminent position in the pantheon, the number of representations of Siva himself is not great. Although statues of Siva with his consort and her sister, as well as statues of Nandin, Siva's mount, have been discovered, Siva was chiefly worshiped by the Khmers in the form of the linga, or fertility rocks (see Plate 52).

We have already noted that even though the Khmers were divided into classes and corporations, these groups did not fight to preserve their own exclusiveness. Working to serve the state, they were a source of strength to the Khmer kings rather than thorns in their flesh. This was the favorable background of the society in which the cult of devaraja was established. This inseparable triumvirate of king, priest, and linga can be understood through inscriptions, particularly the important one of Sdok Kak Thom (SKT). This inscription, found less than twenty-five miles northwest of Sisophon, is written partly in Sanskrit and partly in Khmer. (Khmer was not used in the earliest inscriptions, but in the seventh century, when Tamil, the local language of south India, began to be used for mainland inscriptions, passages in Khmer were also appended to the main Sanskrit texts of Khmer inscriptions. Khmer sections were in prose and the Sanskrit in verse.) The Sanskrit section was regarded by the Khmers as more important, since the Khmer section was cut so that it occupied not more than about a third of the total space. The SKT inscription is inscribed on all four sides of the stone.

The nominal purpose of the SKT inscription was the dedication of a linga by the guru Sadasiva, a brother-in-law of Suryavarman I who also served Udayadityavarman II. At pains to demonstrate that his family had served the Khmer kings ever since Jayavarman II became established at Angkor in 802, he set out a brief history of how the devaraja was established by Jayavarman II, of the part played by his own ancestors, and of the rewards which various Khmer kings bestowed on his family from time to time. Luckily for posterity, Sadasiva decided to record the purely historical section in Khmer as well as in Sanskrit. The parallel account of the same events in two languages, apart from some minor variations in the text, fixes the titles of kings beyond doubt.

The original devaraja ceremony took place, as we have seen, on Phnom Kulen, the Mount Mahendra of Jayavarman II. There were five stages in the ceremony—initiation, study of the sciences, secret rites, ritual celebrations, and distribution of offerings. Hiranyadama, who performed the ceremony, is said by the SKT inscription to have followed four sacred texts. The manuscripts of these texts have perished, and with them the secret of Java's kings. However, three have been located by name in a list of texts cited by the author of a tantric manuscript found in Nepal. The title of one text means literally "The Beheading." Perhaps part of this ceremony was the ritual beheading of a statue representing the king's enemies. Human sacrifice did not take place, but the memory of it was preserved at the ceremony. The fourth text, the *Vinasikha*, which according to the SKT inscription was the most important, has not been located in any list of manuscripts either on the Indian mainland or in Indochina. By following his instructions carefully, Hiranyadama caused the essence of Jayavarman II to enter into the linga, thus creating the steadfast *devaraja* ("god-king"), as it was called in Sanskrit, and the *kamraten jagat ta raja* ("Lord of the Universe who is the King"), as it is written in Khmer. This was how the foundation stone of Angkor's greatness was seen in religious terms and how the linga in particular fitted into the system.

The unique nature of the devaraja ceremony as recounted on the SKT inscription has lost some of its singularity since the discovery of an inscription from southeast Cambodia that refers to another ceremony, hitherto unknown, which Jayavarman II had performed "to prevent Kambujádesa being seized by Java." Doubtless, the king held many such ceremonies, knowledge of which has not survived. Nevertheless, the ceremony performed by Hiranyadama still retains its crucial importance.

The devaraja could be moved from place to place. We have seen how Jayavarman II did not linger on Mount Mahendra but took the Khmer palladium back to Hariharalaya in the plain. When a king died, the new devaraja had to be established and another inseparable triumvirate of king, linga, and high priest founded. In practice, the choice of king depended on which Khmer prince could seize power, but, in theory, son succeeded father. The kind of linga which a new king would found depended on personal taste. One king founded a gold linga. The choice of priest was governed by the order of Jayavarman II and

Hiranyadama that a certain family should maintain the cult of the devaraja. After several generations, however, there was an embarrassingly large number of persons qualified to perform the task who wished to be rewarded. It may be that Sadasiva's qualifications were questioned by a rival and that this was one of the reasons why he set out his genealogy so fully in the SKT inscription. If the Khmer throne were taken by a usurper, he might require the authorized high priest to legalize his position by performing a devaraja ceremony.

The king whose essence had created the devaraja was all-powerful. He was the sole ruler of his empire, the only arbiter in the disputes of his subjects, commander in chief of the armed forces, and the god whom all were expected to worship. He was, moreover, the divinely descended inheritor of his throne, the divinely incarnated personification on earth of Siva, Vishnu, or Brahma. The devaraja could do no wrong, but he was also expected to be a successful emperor who would defeat his country's enemies and reward his subjects with prosperity. He did this by building temple-mountains and by digging reservoirs which would irrigate the land. The security of the kingdom depended on the captains of militia, who in turn looked to the king for help in developing their land.

Within this general framework the Khmer kings expressed certain preferences in the selection of Hindu deities whom they chose to patronize. Sivaism was the most favored religion, especially in the first two centuries of Khmer rule at Angkor. Vishnuism was also favored, while Buddhism existed sporadically as a less important religion until the third and fourth centuries of Khmer rule at Angkor (eleventh to thirteenth centuries A.D.), when it came into its own. The existence of these three religions side by side was made possible by eclecticism (the selecting of pleasing parts from different religions) and syncretism (the combining of different religions). For example, Yasovarman I favored certain deities from the Hindu pantheon, most of whom were associated with Siva but one of whom was Vishnu under the commonly used name Narayana. Jayavarman V employed a Vishnuite teacher whose son was a learned Sivaite. Suryavarman II practiced a particularly mystical brand of Vishnuism, but during the same period gifts could be simultaneously presented to Siva, Vishnu, and Buddha and be recorded on the same inscription.

The amalgamation of Vishnu and Siva was achieved early in Khmer history as is indicated by statues of Harihara. Hara is a name by which Siva is known, and Hari a name for Vishnu. A Harihara found at Phnom Da (Angkor Borei) holds a rosary and, possibly, a trident on the right (Sivaite) side, and a club on the left (Vishnuite) side. Another Harihara found on the same site wears a garment neatly divided down the middle, with a tiger's skin showing a tiger's head on the Sivaite side and traditional drapery on the Vishnuite side, where a discus is held. Harihara continued to be popular in the ninth century. The Khmers' pleasure in Harihara was characteristic of the way in which they absorbed Hinduism. Siva did not exclude Vishnu, nor did Vishnu exclude Siva.

We have not yet said anything about Buddhism except that it came to Indochina with the early Hindu settlers. Unlike the gods of the Hindu trinity, Buddha was a historical figure. The religion associated with his name was so successful that Hinduism claimed Buddha as the ninth incarnation of Vishnu. He was born of a princely family in the middle of the sixth century B.C., and lived a normal life until suddenly as a young married man he was constrained by the sight of human suffering to retire from the world in which he moved. He lived for six years as an ascetic, obtained what he called enlightenment at Bodh-Gaya, and spent the rest of his life teaching. He died— that is to say, according to the Buddhists, he passed into Nirvana—in about 483 B.C., at a ripe old age. In origin, Buddhism was a reformed sect of Hinduism with an emphasis on the problem of pain. Buddha had lived in animal, bird, and human form many previous times. This idea of transmigration and reincarnation was not new to Hinduism. It was a key Hindu belief. Nor was the concept of Nirvana exclusive to Buddhism. The evolution of Buddhism is a paradox. Unlike the founders of other religions, Buddha did not claim that he himself was either God or the son of God. Paradoxically, he came to be worshiped as a god—especially at Angkor.

The philosophy of suffering and pessimism which we associate with Buddhism did not come to Angkor until a much later period. Theravada Buddhism (Teaching of the Elders), also known as Hinayana (Little Vehicle), or Southern school, carried the seeds of pessimism later sown among the Khmers. But in the golden years of the Khmer civilization Buddha was worshiped as a god alongside the Hindu trinity, in accordance with the less pessimistic teachings of Mahayana Buddhism (Greater Vehicle, or Northern school). Suffering did not play the predominant role. The Khmers wanted to reach Nirvana and obtain release from their sufferings, but the prescribed method was to ask certain bodhisattvas (future Buddhas) to intercede on their behalf rather than to pursue Buddha-like asceticism. There were, of course, professional monks living in hermitages, but the idea of being an ascetic did not affect the common people. The Khmers simply regarded the various bodhisattvas as additional spirits in the Hindu pantheon. Although Mahayana Buddhism was a force acting against Hinduism in mainland India, a conflict on the Indian model never really developed in Cambodia. A period of iconoclasm against Buddhism did occur sometime after the reign of Jayavarman VII, but measured on the scale of many centuries of peaceful coexistence between Buddhism and the Hindu religions, this one outbreak of violence is minor. The greatest uniting factor among the Khmers was the cult of the devaraja. As long as the god-king occupied his all-powerful place, the simultaneous worship of Siva, Vishnu, and Buddha took place in amity. The coming of Theravada Buddhism in the thirteenth century was to upset this balance.

In Khmer art Buddha is usually represented sitting in an attitude of meditation, with the serpent Mucilinda protecting him from the elements with his many heads. It is easy to see why the Khmers liked this particular portrayal of Buddha. The serpent was already an integral part of their beliefs, both as the lord of the waters, dating back to early times, and as the means whereby the ocean could be churned to produce ambrosia. Ancient Khmer Buddhist statues are robust and immobile, and in the reign of Jaya-

varman VII they have an enigmatic smile (see Plate 40).
The slender, elongated Buddhas seen in Indochina today
date from a period when the Khmers had abandoned Angkor and were under Thai influence. Among the many bodhisattvas portrayed by the Khmers the most popular was
Avalokitesvara, usually known under the name Lokesvara,
a deity associated with healing and compassion (see Plate
13).

Buddhism was so well integrated into the fabric of
Khmer religion that eventually it merged with the cult of
the devaraja. We are, of course, still speaking of Mahayana Buddhism and not Theravada, which would eventually undermine the devaraja. The idea of the devaraja was
the essence of the king's power, whether he personally was
regarded as the incarnation of Siva or Vishnu or Brahma.
The final amalgamation of the devaraja with Mahayana
Buddhism occurred when a Buddhist king, Jayavarman
VII, installed a *buddharaja*, a statue of Buddha, instead of
the linga. The idea and the characteristics of the devaraja
—power, divine authority, and inability to do wrong—
were present, but the *raja* (king) instead of being a *deva*
(Hindu god) was Buddha. This syncretism would be surprising if it were not for the fact that Buddhism, Hinduism, and the idea of the devaraja had existed for so long
side by side.

Khmer religion and art were also peopled with a large
number of minor deities and supernatural beings. These
less important personages, of whom Ganeca and Garuda
have already been mentioned, were immensely popular
with the common people. The Khmers were not sun-wor-
shipers, but Surya, the sun-god, was among the minor deities whom they respected. Indra, the Hindu god of the
sky, was worshiped as the bringer of rain, but he did not
occupy as important a place as Vishnu or Siva. There is a
passage in the *Ramayana* which describes spirits in the
shape of bears and cats, with heads of tigers and panthers,
and sporting the beaks of crows and parrots. The Khmers
called these spirits Yakshas and used them as guardians
(*dvarapalas*) of temples. Other guardians included Nandin, the sacred ox of Siva. Besides the many sandstone

statues of Nandin and the Nandin-type pedestals which
have been discovered, a gold-leaf Nandin was used as part
of the sacred deposit under a brick tower at Angkor, and
a bronze foot of Nandin has been discovered at Banteay
Srei. Of the many other spirits depicted in Khmer sculpture, the favorable ones are classed as *devas* (gods)—as,
for example, in the churning legend—and the unfavorable
ones as Rakshasas or *asuras* (demons). Female deities
were represented by the Apsarases, celestial dancers seen
in large numbers on the upper walls of Angkor Wat, and by
*devatas* (goddesses). The total number of these minor
spirits as bequeathed to us by the Khmer sculptors far ex-
ceeds that of the lingas. We should, therefore, guard
against an impression that the Khmers were obsessed with
their phallic palladium, even though it was the ultimate
thing in their lives. They liked the beaks of Garuda and of
the Yakshas. The bedecked headdresses of the Apsarases
pleased them. Surya's two horses were nobly depicted. The
gods of Hinduism can be seen riding their various mounts
—Brahma on his goose, for example—along the ancient
Khmer friezes. There is gaiety and warmth in the artist's
feeling for his gods.

The Khmers acted according to their beliefs. There was
no gap between work and worship, for work *was* worship.
Worship was not just saying a prayer to a divine being or
lighting incense; it was actually being in a divine universe.
The Khmer peasant climbing the steps to his house felt
himself to be an eternal part of the universe: in place,
since his habitation was related to the temple of the devaraja at Angkor; and in time, because he was traveling
from one existence to another, and eventually, so he
hoped, to Nirvana. And yet this kind of worship was almost without meaning because the meaning was so highly
organized. The worshipers could never stand back from
the images and assess their real worth. The Khmer's duty
was to a great religious ideal which he had not formed
himself and which he could not change. While the devaraja reigned supreme, either as a statue or linga on the
temple-mountain, the structure of Angkor's civilization
lasted. The lower strata of Khmer society did not question

their own beliefs or vary the strenuous activity which the god-kings required of them.

At Angkor there was no secular education. Children were instructed by monks and priests, but such instruction was not intended to liberate them or broaden their horizons. In the Khmers' golden age priests came into the houses of the laity to perform ceremonies to insure that the grip of religion was never relaxed. The piece of white cotton around a priest's neck was his surety that crowds would make way for him in the city and that the villagers would receive him with respect in the countryside. Besides the priests, there were many sorcerers with alleged healing powers and astronomers who predicted eclipses and the occurrence of prodigies.

An inscription of Yasovarman I at Prasat Komnap gives a clear picture of how a Vishnuite temple was organized in the late ninth century. This particular temple was called Vaisnavasrama, which means literally the *asram* (hermitage) of Vishnu. It was located near the laterite ruins of Prasat Komnap at Angkor, where the inscription was found. The ruins lie between the ancient Khmer road from Angkor Thom to the east, and the south bank of the East Baray reservoir. The temple is about a third of a mile from the reservoir, which is referred to in the inscription by its normal name, Yasodharatataka. The presence of at least fifty slaves in Vaisnavasrama indicates that it was not as small as the word "hermitage" suggests. Monastery is a better description. The director, referred to as *kuladhyaksa* and *kulapati,* was responsible for increasing the monastery's wealth and for protecting its inmates. He also gave hospitality, especially to the king and the king's retinue of women. During these royal sojourns the women of the king's retinue were not allowed to visit the inmates in their Vishnuite cells. The inmates were, in fact, prohibited from having any contact with women inside the precincts—not excluding their own wives. It was quite possible to enter the monastery for a period and then return to normal life.

The director of Vaisnavasrama, who could actually refuse hospitality to women known to be of low repute, had a duty to care for the old, the young, and the sick. Moreover, during the rainy season he had to provide lodging and one meal a day for visiting Vishnuites. At the full moon of Tapasya (February–March) he had to feed visitors who came to bathe ceremonially in the East Baray. The monastery could also provide sanctuary for people on the run who claimed they were innocent. The killing of inoffensive creatures, presumably human as well as animal, was prohibited near the precincts of the monastery and the East Baray. The inmates received subsistence, the most important items of which seem to have been toothpicks, betel nuts, rice, and betel leaves. The director, who was assisted by a sacrificer (*yajvan*) and a teacher (*adhyapaka*), was entitled to one female slave, nine male slaves, and ten agricultural workers. The teacher had ten servants to assist him. While the director's authority extended over the inmates at all times, they could retire to their cells, where they were regarded as being off duty and not on call. The director himself was controlled by an official of the royal household. If he disobeyed the decrees set out in the monastery's charter—if, for example, he embezzled religious funds—then he would be punished by the king. The exact punishment was not clearly stated. If an outsider seized the monastery's goods, he would go straight to hell. The picture which emerges of this monastery is of a well operated, smoothly run organism. Although the support of such institutions placed a heavy burden on the Khmers, they were at least run efficiently.

Vaisnavasrama was a small temple. The 1191 inscription of Preah Khan (Angkor) gives a full, though not always clear, idea of the time, money, and materials which went into the maintenance of a large temple. A thousand persons were lodged there, and many thousands more were involved in carrying out its charter. Festivals were ordained on the fifth, eighth, twelfth, fourteenth, and fifteenth days of every half-month, together with a feast at the new year and eighteen other special feast days. There must have been 135 festivals at Preah Khan every year. In other words, one was held about every third day. The amount of time thus consumed in religious festivals is alarming. Nor was this peculiar to Preah Khan. The inscription of Ta Prohm, a comparable temple, also lists a number of festivals, though the total is in fact less than at Preah Khan.

Goods for Preah Khan (Angkor) were supplied from two sources—the villages and the royal storehouses. Provisions included rice, sesame, chick-peas, butter, curds, fresh milk, honey, molasses, oil of sesame, vegetables, fruit, pepper, and salt. Rough goods included styrax, oleoresin of pine (there are a few pine trees on Cambodian hills), eaglewood, wax, santal, camphor, silks, beds, white and red cloth to cloak 283 statues, mosquito nets, cushions, rings, boxes, ewers, and copper bowls. Livestock included 423 goats, 360 pigeons, peacocks, horses, elephants, female slaves, and water buffalo. The temple treasure included gold utensils, diamonds, beryls, rubies, pearls, copper, bronze, tin, lead, and iron. The following item was also required: "one brown cow with its hoofs and horns gilded and furnished with a cover."

We can visualize the busy scenes of Khmers unloading all these materials from boats tied up to the *kompong*. It needs no effort of the imagination to see that the provision of such quantities imposed a strain on the Khmer economy. Only a highly organized system based on the power of the devaraja could withstand the burden. Nevertheless, it is gratifying that all this money and stock did not go to support one religion exclusively. We have seen that Vishnuism, Sivaism, and Buddhism existed side by side at Angkor. The provisions set forth in the Prasat Komnap inscription, which told us about Vaisnavasrama, were repeated almost word for word in a Sivaite inscription (Prasat Prei Prasat) and in a Buddhist inscription (Tep Pranam). These two inscriptions relate to the founding of a Sivaite hermitage (Brahmasrama) and a Buddhist hermitage (Saugatasrama). The Khmers were not exactly broad-minded, but they could achieve a satisfactory syncretism of differing religions. Some of the details of life in the three hermitages differ. For example, the Sivaite inmates have prescribed for them jars of ashes for cleaning the hair of their chignons, a custom well known in India, where ashes instead of water are used by certain sects for washing. The ashes are regarded as a sign of Siva, and washing in them is an act of purification. Cinders are still regarded in Cambodia as a medicinal substance with which the skin can be purified. Another example of divergence between life in one hermitage and that in another is to be found in the Buddhist inscription, which significantly omits the appointment of a sacrificer. It is the similarity of regimes, not the differences, which is so striking, however. The Khmers did not mind switching from one religion to another—as long as the idea of the devaraja was not undermined.

## DOMESTIC LIFE

The basic Khmer costume for both sexes was a self-fastening rectangle of cloth wrapped around the hips; the upper body was naked. The men's garment came halfway down their thighs, and the women wore theirs to their ankles, with bust exposed. But the garment could be small or large, and there were endless variations in how it could be arranged. After the garment was tucked between the legs and knotted at the waist, the spare cloth could be pleated or knotted or flounced or looped. A piece of jewelry might be added, but whether this was a gold clasp or a diamond-studded belt, it was not essential for keeping the basic garment in place. Only when additional scarflike pieces were added, might a brooch be needed to hold them together, perhaps in cross-gartered fashion or else in a series of twists. Khmer sculptors featured pleats and loops in extravagant ways, but the real Khmers dressed more simply than some of the carved figures would have us think. As a rule the people went barefoot and did not wear hats. The Khmer women liked gold bracelets, bangles, and necklaces. Hair was normally worn in a chignon.

A Cambodian proverb says, "When you are asleep at

night, do not talk with your wife." [2] Because Cambodian houses are perched on stilts, anyone crouching under such a house can listen to privately uttered indiscretions. The Khmers also built their houses on stilts. Although fragments of stilts have been found on the royal palace site of Angkor Thom, none of the stone or brick ruins which have survived was used for living purposes. The Khmer house has yet to be reconstructed with success. Those structures pictured on bas-reliefs are confusing. The artist abolishes the walls and shows only doors, windows, and pillars. Scenes are not carved in depth. This means that the foreground is carved at the bottom of the frieze and the background at the top. There is no satisfactory way of interpreting these sculptured houses, but the Khmer house must have been similar to the Cambodian dwelling.

Houses were made entirely of wood. They were roofed with palm leaves, most often with the spiky leaves of the sugar palm. At the beginning of the dry season, about November, the young Khmers shinned up the trees and cut down branches of leaves five or six feet long. Palm swifts nesting on the underside of these leaves were rudely disturbed. Branches thus obtained were made supple by long soaking in water. The women or young girls split each branch down the center along the stalk and sewed the individual leaves to bamboo slats. In this manner they assembled rectangles, which were the components of the roof. When the open area was fully covered by these rectangles, a bamboo trellis was added to prevent them from blowing away in a high wind. Similar rectangles of palm leaves and bamboo slats were used for walls and partitions.

Chou Ta-Kouan gives a convincing description of the inside of a Khmer house. "The ordinary people," he wrote, "have a house, but without table, bench, basin, or bucket. They employ only an earthenware pot for cooking the rice, and employ in addition an earthenware pan for preparing the sauce." [3] The bas-reliefs of the Bayon show

[2] A. Pannetier, "Sentences et proverbes Cambodgiens," *Bulletin de l'École Française d'Extrême-Orient,* Vol. XV. No. 3 (Hanoi, Vietnam, 1915), 51.

[3] Chou Ta-Kouan, p. 30.

Fig. 13  Khmer farmer climbing the sugar palm *(Mavis Cameron)*.

the various cooking pots and jars which the Khmers used in their daily life. Fragments and whole pots recovered in excavations indicate that the Khmers did not excel in ceramics. A rich and discriminating people, they preferred to import foreign pottery. Chou Ta-Kouan writes that Chinese celadons were in demand at Angkor, and many fragments of exportware from China have been found on the Angkor Thom palace site. Khmer pots are not elaborately decorated. They are not unlike the crude cooking pots baked in Cambodia today. Before firing his pot in the kiln, the Cambodian potter recites this prayer: "Oh ancient spirits of the village, help me so that my pots do not break. If they are well cooked, I will offer you some alcohol." [4] Bad spots are recognized by the dull noise they

4 A. Souyris-Roland, "La poterie dans le Sud-Cambodge," *Bulletin de la Societé des Études Indochinoises,* Vol. XXV, No. 3 (Saigon, Vietnam, 1950), 308.

make when tapped. Their brick-red color varies according to the amount of baking—usually one hour—and the amount of iron in the clay. When the pots are used in Cambodian kitchens—the same would have been true at Angkor—their original color soon becomes blackened beyond recognition.

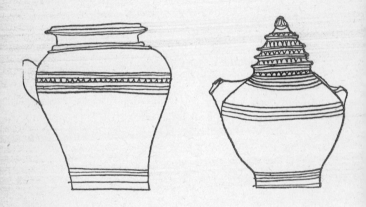

Fig. 14   Pottery—two types from the twelfth century (*Mavis Cameron*).

Chou Ta-Kouan continues his description of a Khmer house as follows: "They bury three stones for a fireplace, and from a coconut shell they make a ladle. To serve rice, they employ Chinese plates, either earthenware or copper. For the sauce, they employ tree leaves of which they make little glasses which, even when full of liquid, do not run out. . . ." Leaves of banana trees were especially good for making containers for food or drink. "In addition," writes Chou Ta-Kouan, "they use the leaves of the *kiao* [?] for making spoons to drain the liquid [in these glasses] and take it to the mouth; when they have finished they throw them down. . . . For sleeping they use only bamboo mats, and they also sleep on the floorboards." [5]   The Khmers usually did not have heavy furniture. Because the floors of their houses were often made of bamboo slats, it was inadvisable to place heavy pieces of furniture upon them. The houses were lighted with wax candles and coconut-oil lamps. Mosquito nets were also used—though not by the majority of the population.

In their furniture and lighting, as in everything else, the Khmer kings must have lived on a completely different scale. Chou Ta-Kouan is not so good a source for descriptions of the royal apartments because we do not know just how much he saw himself. The royal bedchamber, for example, must have been elaborately carved with motifs which the Khmers liked to use: Garuda, the *naga,* and floral patterns. A bronze foot of a throne with a *naga* motif has been found a few miles south of Phnom Penh. It is similar to the foot of Suryavarman II's throne on the bas-reliefs of Angkor Wat. This kind of throne, resembling the preaching chairs from which Buddhist monks give sermons in Cambodia today, would have stood in the royal apartments. The stand of a bronze candelabra has also been found south of Phnom Penh. It would have been furnished with wick and oil so that it gave a good light. Chinese brocades were hung from the apartment walls, and some of the Chinese designs influenced the royal sculptors—in Angkor Wat, for example. Royal reception rooms depicted on the Bayon frieze are hung with embroidered curtains.

Friendship between one Khmer and another depended more on eating together than on drinking. But the meals were very simple. The main staples of the Khmer diet were rice, salt, and fish. Every summer Cambodia becomes a vast feeding ground for fish. In the summer months the swollen waters of the Mekong River cannot escape fast enough to the sea, so they turn landward at Phnom Penh and flow up to the Great Lake. The forest on the borders of the lake becomes inundated, and this is how the fish come to eat the ants, as described in a traditional Cambo-

[5] Chou Ta-Kouan, pp. 30–31.

Fig. 15   A Khmer throne *(Mavis Cameron).*

dian proverb. It is, however, the phytoplankton of the
Great Lake which fattens them. From December until
May, during a period when the waters are calm, the phytoplankton has a chance to grow, making the Great Lake
an ideal feeding ground for the fish. Thousands of tiny fish
come up to the Great Lake with the current from the Mekong River. They include gudgeon, shad, large catfish, sil-
very featherbacks, and even small sharks. Eels are also
plentiful.

It is an easy matter to catch fish in Cambodia, although
Angkor was not the ideal place from which to organize a
fishery. Many inland pools and creeks are flooded each
year by water from the lake. When the waters subside,
these natural ponds are cut off from the main stream and
can be fished. The floods recede at the end of September
and in October. It is now the ants' turn to eat the fish. As
the lake is emptied of its phytoplankton, a great shoal of
fish collects at the mouth of the Mekong River to feed on
it. But as a rule the Khmers did not fish in the sea. There
was no need to. Cambodia itself provided them with an
enormous annual haul of fish, which they dried in the sun
or turned into a sauce.

Salt was needed for preserving fish. Chou Ta-Kouan
says that it was obtainable on the Indochina coast, and in
all probability it came from the Kampot area. There must
also have been a salt route from the coast to Angkor. Al-

Fig. 16   Khmer fisherman throwing his net *(Mavis Cameron)*.

though Chou Ta-Kouan says that the exploitation of salt
was not restricted, at certain periods the Khmers established checkpoints and taxed the movement of salt. A pre-
Angkor inscription found in the Phnom Penh region mentions that at a certain landing-stage quantities of salt had
to be redistributed to boats belonging to six sanctuaries.

Besides the rice, salt, and fish already mentioned, fruit
and venison and pork made up part of the Khmer diet.
Brow-antlered deer, barking deer, hog deer, and the small
mouse deer were plentiful and good to eat. Bananas and
oranges provided the main fruit in their diet. Although
there were many other fruits that are still grown in Cambodia today, guavas were not yet cultivated. Pepper bushes
existed at Angkor, but the planned cultivation of pepper in
Cambodia did not begin until the nineteenth century. Milk
was drunk, a custom which lapsed in Cambodia after the
fall of Angkor because a new religion prohibited the killing of animals. This prohibition, which in practice was not
strictly followed, became illogically extended to the con-
sumption of milk.
Chou Ta-Kouan mentions several kinds of alcohol man-
ufactured by the Khmers, including one made from sugarcane and another from honey. Juice from the sugarcane
was extracted by a press consisting of two vertical grind-
stones, operated by a pair of elephants pulling on hawsers.
This process is depicted on a bas-relief of Banteay

Chhmar. Honey was not easily obtainable in the Angkor region. An inscription in the time of Udayadityavarman II suggests that the Plaine des Joncs became an important center for the collection of honey. In more recent times Rach-Gia has become a favorite haunt of bees. They build large nests high up in trees or on rocks. Fires are lighted under these aerial hives and the inmates expelled by the smoke. After three or four months the bees tend to abandon their centers and seek new ones. Cambodians study the bees' nomadic habits and seek out the remotest apiaries. The Khmers, who used beeswax in hair dressings, did likewise.

We have seen how the Khmers dressed, what kind of houses they had, and what they ate. But to enter their domestic life more intimately we need to know about the landscape in which they moved, about the weather, and about the tiny incidents which make up domestic life in any age. As they went about their daily business, the Khmers moved in a landscape of contrasting greens. The green of the banana trees was dull, and the green of rice seedlings glossy. The sky above was not always a brilliant blue. At certain times of the year the blue seemed almost white, even in a cloudless sky. The Cambodian equivalent for "Don't count your chickens before they're hatched" is "Because you hear thunder, do not rush to throw away your water." For the Khmers, the sound of thunder toward the end of the dry season did not necessarily mean that rain was going to fall. Even when thunder sounded on high, they had to wait patiently for the rain, conserving their jars of stale water, the breeding grounds for mosquitoes.

The hell scene of Angkor Wat's bas-reliefs shows victims shivering in the cold. November and December are the coolest months in Cambodia. At night, and especially just before dawn, the temperature drops sharply; the peasants shiver in their houses on stilts. But ice and snow were completely unknown to the Khmers. When Henri Mouhot, the rediscoverer of Angkor, was traveling across Indochina, he amazed his guides with stories of how he had known of rivers completely frozen over (i.e., the Neva in Leningrad, where he once worked as a tutor). Snow sometimes falls in the extreme north of Indochina, but the Khmer empire never extended that far.

The Khmers valued their teeth as heirlooms. An inscription found near Kompong Cham says that a certain eighty-year-old man founded a linga in the place and at the same time deposited all his teeth there. Either he had been collecting these as they fell out, or they were roughly extracted from his mouth during a long life. Homely incidents of this kind help put the life of the Khmers in perspective.

## LITERARY TASTE

A literary atmosphere existed both inside and outside the temples. The priests were literate and sophisticated. Since the common people looked up to the priests, the ordinary Khmer also took on a dash of sophistication. He too learned passages from the Hindu epics and discussed stories of Vishnu with his friends. Evidence shows that Angkor had libraries and an ample stock of manuscripts. An inscription of the mid-eleventh century mentions the Khmer king as editor of some texts. An inscription of Banteay Srei records that the younger brother of the king's teacher copied certain texts to prevent their loss to posterity. Another inscription refers to a collection of manuscripts in a hermitage during the time of Jayavarman VI. Those who destroyed manuscripts were threatened with eternal damnation, a fate which book burners and looters of libraries thoroughly deserve. For the Khmers, manuscripts were objects with a religious value, which explains the severe penalty.

Manuscripts were stored in subsidiary buildings within the enclosures of Khmer temples. Normally there were two of these buildings, one for the half-month period of the waxing moon and the other for the half-month period of the waning moon. The sacred texts, regarded as part of a temple's goods, could be stored in libraries along with many other sacred possessions. Throughout Khmer epigraphy this temple property is divided into two sections for use during the alternate half-months of the waxing and waning moons. Thus, two library buildings were constructed in each Khmer temple, but they were rather more than libraries, in our sense of the term.

Khmer manuscripts themselves have perished, but the language of the inscriptions on stone indicates that the Khmers had a true sense of literary style. An inscription of Suryavarman I contains sixty-one virtuoso stanzas in which the king is praised. The style is sometimes overdone, and another inscription, praising Dharanindravarman I, is surpassingly silly; for example, Stanza III of Face A:

There was a king whose splendid feet were illuminated by the brilliance of the gems which held in their diadem the crown of kings giving him homage, sun among kings reigning on earth, raised in the sky from the line of the kings' kings.[6]

But other inscriptions, like that of Baksei Chamkrong, which gives a resumé of Khmer history, are more restrained:

In this line was born the happy and most glorious Jayavarman [II], who established his residence on the summit of Mahendra [Phnom Kulen], who conquered the god of a hundred sacrifices [Indra], and whose footstool became the touchstone of royal diadems. . . . (Stanza XIX) [7]

An inscription in a corner tower of the wall at Angkor Thom refers to Jayavarman VII in the following terms:

[6] George Coedès, ed., *Inscriptions du Cambodge*, Vol. VI, Paris, 1954, p. 306.

[7] Coedès, Vol. IV, Paris, 1952, p. 97.

In his mandates, as in all things, this logician con-
formed to the logic which is well known from the
knowledge of rivers. As in battle, he broke those who
resisted him, but not those who bent like rattan. . . .
(Stanza LXXXIX) [8]

The Khmer lapidaries, writing chiefly in Sanskrit, drew
their inspiration from the Sanskrit models of India. But
from a literary point of view the Sanskrit literature of
Cambodia, though not copious, is important to Sanskrit
scholars in its own right. The Khmers did not copy Indian
writings slavishly.

Puns and word play were not uncommon. For example,
where the author of an inscription intends to say that the
king sated the crows with the entrails of his enemies, he
refers to the enemy partisans by a word which means both
partisan and bird. Ability to pun in this way or to compose Sanskrit verses was a much sought after skill at Angkor. Scholars were highly regarded. Jayavarman VI once
held a colloquium to which he invited the leading scholars
of the kingdom in order that they might question an up-
and-coming young scholar-priest. One of the wives of Jayavarman VII became chief lecturer in a Buddhist foundation. Although this literary atmosphere pervaded the
Khmer court, and literary ability was highly valued, we
must admit that the language of the inscriptions is sometimes an obstacle. All the kings and queens of Angkor
cannot have been as brilliant, as compassionate, and as
splendid as they are described on these lumps of sandstone.

Although the manuscripts themselves have perished, we
know some of the ways in which the Khmers wrote and
the materials they used. There are frequent references in
the inscriptions to slaves who "make leaves," that is, who
prepare palm leaves for use as writing materials. Chou
Ta-Kouan refers to books made of "palm leaves piled up
very regularly," and the books illustrated on the bas-reliefs
answer this description.[9] The making of palm-leaf manu-

[8] *Ibid.*, p. 228.
[9] Chou Ta-Kouan, p. 15.

scripts has dwindled in present-day Cambodia, although artisans working in several Buddhist monasteries will do the job. Sheets varying in size were threaded together by twine passed through two holes, and were then clamped between two pieces of wood. The wood was painted with scenes from the book. A sharp-pointed instrument was needed to scratch letters on palm leaf. Such a tool has not been excavated, but any bronze or ivory point would have been effective. After the letters were etched, a black dye was added to make the writing stand out from the pale sheets.

Chou Ta-Kouan has a section on writing materials in which he says that skins were also used. Until recently the Cambodians made a kind of paper from tree bark, dyed it black, and wrote on it in chalk. This writing material, which Chou Ta-Kouan mistook for skin, probably existed in ancient times too. "Ordinary writings," he says, "like official documents, are always written on the skins of stags or deer and analogous materials which they dye black. Depending on their length and breadth, each person cuts them to suit his taste. The people use a sort of powder which resembles chalk from China, and they make it in sticks. . . . Holding the stick in their hands, they write on pieces of skin. . . . If they rub on something wet, [the characters] rub out." Chou Ta-Kouan also remarks somewhat humorously that when the people have finished writing they put the piece of chalk on their ear. Letters read from left to right and not from top to bottom. "For their petitions," he adds, "there are also booths of writers where they are written." [10]

Although Chou Ta-Kouan states that the Khmers did not have seals, several have been discovered. The head of a bronze seal in the form of a bearded man was found in a province of Thailand (Ubon), and a complete bronze seal was discovered in the Battambang region of Cambodia. This second seal is in the form of a dragonlike animal eating a human figure. Both seals are inscribed with a single Khmer verb meaning "guard." A rock crystal seal has been unearthed at Phnom Bakheng. If these were royal seals, then Chou Ta-Kouan would not have seen them in use. They might have been utilized for sealing a safe-conduct pass from the Khmer king or, more mundanely, as an indication that documents stamped "guard" were to be filed in the royal archives. There were officials at Angkor whose special care was to look after the king's documents. Our knowledge of the Khmers would be greatly increased if any such documents could be found, and the discovery of the Dead Sea scrolls leads one to hope that some may yet be discovered, but this is not an expectation which most people entertain seriously.

One of the most common manuscripts at Angkor would have been of the Hindu epic poem the *Ramayana*. The Khmers even regarded its author, Valmiki, as a kind of deity, and their neighbors, the Chams, actually started a cult of Valmiki. At Angkor a Khmer priest called Kavindrapandita mastered the *Ramayana* and taught it. Public recitations also took place. The Khmers believed that anyone who read or recited the *Ramayana* was guaranteed some kind of spiritual blessing. For the Cambodians the characters of the *Ramayana* have assumed all kinds of duties—as cardinal and intercardinal points of the compass, for example. Hanuman, the monkey general, represents the northeast. From before the beginning of the Angkor period until the present day, the inhabitants of Cambodia, as well as other peoples of Southeast Asia, have taken a special liking to the *Ramayana*. Since Rama was an incarnation of Vishnu, it was natural that the Vishnuite temple of Angkor Wat should be decorated with scenes from the *Ramayana*. We have also seen that sculptures based on this epic tale were executed in other parts of Cambodia, too. At Koh Ker there was a sculptured duel between the two monkeys, Sugriva and Valin.

The Cambodians have manuscripts of the *Ramayana* which in all probability were derived from ancient Khmer writings. Apart from the fact that their origin cannot definitely be traced back to the Khmers, the manuscripts are also in a pitiable fragmentary state. François Martini, a specialist in Khmer, has compared the fragments of the

Cambodian *Ramayana* (known as the *Ream Ker*) with the bas-reliefs of Angkor Wat. He has also compared the *Ream Ker* with Valmiki's *Ramayana* as it is known on the Indian mainland. The result is extremely interesting because he found that the *Ream Ker* differed in certain details from the Indian *Ramayana* and that these differences were also to be found on the bas-reliefs. In the northwest corner pavilion of Angkor Wat, Rama is depicted shooting at a target with his bow. The Indian version of the *Ramayana* does not speak of Rama actually using the bow but only of his breaking it, whereas the *Ream Ker* says three times that Rama shot the bow himself. In a different panel of the same pavilion, Rama and Lakshman are shown with bows. In the corresponding scene in the Indian *Ramayana* they are armed with swords. The *Ream Ker,* following the bas-relief, says they fought with bows. The Khmer version of Rama's saga, which finds echoes in the later *Ream Ker,* was the Khmers' individual contribution to epic poetry.

The *Mahabharata,* scenes from which also figure on the bas-reliefs of Angkor Wat, was not quite as popular as the *Ramayana.* It was known to the Khmers before they settled at Angkor. A seventh-century inscription relates the donation of a manuscript comprising a chapter from the *Mahabharata.* The Kiratarjuniya episode, which describes a contest between Siva disguised as a Kirata (mountaineer) and Arjuna, was particularly popular. It occurs in the bas-reliefs of Angkor Wat, Banteay Srei, Baphuon, and Prasat Khna Sen Keo. The last-named temple, east of Koh Ker near the west slopes of Mount Tbeng, has a panel in which two hunters point their bows at a wild boar. The left-hand hunter is Siva, the right-hand hunter, Arjuna, and the boar an evil spirit who is trying to kill Arjuna but who is eventually killed by Siva. There is a simplicity in this panel which is absent from the writhing masses of figures on the walls of Angkor Wat.

Besides these two epic poems, the Khmers possessed many other religious texts. Those which were used to perform the devaraja ceremony have already been mentioned. An eleventh-century inscription mentions a recitation of the *Vishnudharma,* a text well known in India. An inscription of Banteay Srei refers to a text which has been identified with a commentary by the Indian grammarian Panini.

An inscription of Banteay Kdei names a text which corresponds to the name of a well-known tantra in India. Obviously these texts and many others were important in regulating the religious life of the Khmers. A priest of Harshavarman II is described as performing the rites of a Sivaite cult in accordance with the sacred texts. Chou Ta-Kouan, who also noted the existence of such books, did not himself know their titles or attend recitations.

Judging from Cambodian stories, we must conclude that the Khmers were great storytellers, too. In addition to religious texts and the epic poems, there must have existed a great body of folklore and legends, all of which has perished. We know from the bas-reliefs that the Khmers had a sense of comedy and tragedy. The tropical climate must be blamed for the fact that written folktales, bursting with comic and tragic situations, have disappeared.

## COMMERCE

The Khmers were not a race of traders like their Funanese predecessors, but the wealth of Angkor nevertheless attracted merchants from the outside world, especially from China. While Chinese chronicles are often uncertain sources for Khmer history, their lists of goods which could be obtained in Cambodia are much more reliable. The Chinese merchants, some of whom lived at Angkor, were less likely to make mistakes about merchandise which affected their pockets than about the Khmer civilization itself.

Chou Ta-Kouan's mission to Angkor at the end of the thirteenth century was probably commercial. He was much struck by the fact that among the Khmers women took charge of commerce. Bas-reliefs of the Bayon show women seated at market stalls with cakes, fish, and other food for sale. Payment would be made in rice or in cloth.

The market opened at six o'clock in the morning and closed at midday. There were no regular shops, but each female hawker would have her appointed place. Wares were spread out on mats or placed on low tables. The Khmer king charged rent for the space occupied by each stall. When a Chinese merchant arrived at Angkor, his first concern was to recruit a Khmer fishwife who would help him in his commercial transactions.

The Chinese brought with them merchandise which they knew the Khmers liked to buy. Gold and silver were in demand, and flower-patterned silks were also popular. Chou Ta-Kouan did some market research on this subject and found that a particular kind of flower-patterned material was confined to the priests and the royal family. The cotton material, from which the ordinary Khmer made the rectangular clothing for his loins, was imported from India and Champa. The Thais also exported cloth to Angkor, but not in the first three or four centuries of Khmer rule there. Judging from the bas-reliefs, we can see that the patterns favored by the Khmers were not complex; they particularly liked a simple arrangement of open lotus flowers. Silks from China, as well as gold and silver, were used for currency.

Other objects in demand from China included mercury, vermilion, paper, sulfur, saltpeter, sandalwood, angelica, musk, canvas, lacquered plates, and pewter. The Khmers also bought umbrellas, iron pots, copper plates, pearls, eel pots, baskets, wooden combs, and mats. It is odd to learn that the Khmers imported objects like baskets and mats, which they could perfectly well have made themselves. The reason must have been that the Khmers were wealthy and could afford to import such things. They were not compelled to buy goods from China. On their side, the Chinese sometimes restricted the export of goods—beans and corn for example—which the Khmers wanted.

The Khmers had various products which the Chinese, in turn, imported. The feathers of kingfishers were eagerly sought by the Chinese, and Sir Osbert Sitwell once suggested happily that the Khmer empire eventually collapsed because the supply of kingfishers ran out. "Cambodian kingfishers," he wrote, "were esteemed above all others in the Chinese market, because of their superior sheen and coloring. . . . No wonder, either, that these towers and cornices [of Angkor Wat] tend to aspire, to take to themselves the angle and shape of wings, for on wings they were built, and out of wings they came. . . ." [11] "This celebrated theory is not to be taken seriously, but the Chinese writers do in fact speak at length about Cambodian kingfishers and of how they were caught.

Chau Ju-Qua, quoting from the *Ling-wai-tai-ta*, writes:

> Kingfishers' feathers are got in great quantities in Cambodia, where [the birds] are brought forth in nests built by the side of lakes or ponds in the depths of the hills. Each pond is the home of just one male and one female bird; the intrusion of a third bird always ends in a duel to the death. The natives, taking advantage of this peculiarity, rear decoy birds, and walk about with one sitting on the raised left hand. The birds in their nests, noticing the intruder, make for the [bird on the] hand to fight it, quite ignoring the presence of the man, who, with his right hand, covers them with a net and thus makes them prisoners without fail.[12]

There were also other methods of catching kingfishers. The Khmer hunter would lie in wait near a pool where kingfishers came to look for fish. A female bird would be exposed to view in a cage. When another bird approached, it would be caught in a net. At one point during the Sung dynasty the Chinese emperor forbade the killing of kingfishers, but according to Chau Ju-Qua, feathers were still smuggled into China in the lining of merchants' clothing. This trade helped the Khmers pay for their imports.

Cardamon was grown by the tribal population living in the Cardamon Mountains, south of Battambang. The Khmers exploited trade in cardamon as do the present-day Cambodians. There were many more elephants then than there are today, and ivory was a valuable export.

[11] Osbert Sitwell, *Escape with Me,* London, 1939, pp. 140–41.

[12] Chau Ju-Qua, *Records of Foreign Nations,* trans. by Friedrich Hirth and W. W. Rockhill, St. Petersburg, Russia, 1911, p. 235.

Chou Ta-Kouan mentions a number of natural products which were also important: rare woods, resin, beeswax, and rhinoceros horn. The Khmers made ropes and containers for merchandise from the many different rattans which were available in the forest. They were not famed for their rope-making. Some of the rattans—the *calamus usitatus,* for example—were pliant and good for cording purposes, but did not last long. There was no fleet to carry Khmer products to foreign ports. The economic effort of the country was concentrated on producing rice. As long as rice production kept pace with the expanding population and nothing interfered with the irrigation systems the Khmer economy remained viable. Chinese merchants found that a visit to Angkor or even a prolonged residence there was well worth their while. When the Khmers declined, almost every commercial activity passed gradually into the hands of the Chinese.

## FESTIVALS

Cambodian customs like the tug-of-war and the building of pyramidal sand castles at New Year's go back far in time and are connected with the growth of crops. These customs, which the Khmers had too, were intended to make the rain fall. The rain duly fell and the rice grew. Then an agrarian festival took place. Chou Ta-Kouan describes it as follows: "In the seventh month they burn the rice. At this moment the new rice is ripe; they go to look for it outside the south gate, and they burn it like an offering to the Buddha. Very many people go by cart or elephant to attend this ceremony, but the king stays at home." The absence of the king from the agrarian festival suggests that it originated in the Khmers' tribal days. The festival took place not only at Angkor but throughout the Khmer empire. An inscription mentions a certain part of the temple precinct at Preah Vihear where "one burns the

1. Angkor Wat: general view from a gateway on the western causeway.

2. Angkor Wat: a bud-shaped tower.

3. Angkor Wat: the west gopura.

4. Angkor Wat: the moat, part of an ancient irrigation system, now in danger of being blocked with water hyacinth.

5. Angkor Wat: detail from the famous frieze of bas-reliefs.

6. Angkor Wat: seen from the summit of Phnom Bakheng.

7. Angkor Wat: an engraving of the facade based on a drawing by
Henri Mouhot, the rediscoverer of Angkor.

8. Angkor Wat: smiling female figures from the upper courtyard.

9. Angkor Thom: Victory Gateway (Royal Embassy of Cambodia in London).

10. Angkor Thom: a giant head, detail from the churning of the Sea of Milk sculptures.

11. Angkor Thom: the Bayon, general view.

12. Angkor Thom (the Bayon): a head of Lokesvara, possibly damaged by iconoclasts.

13. Angkor Thom (the Bayon): a head of Lokesvara.

14. Angkor Thom (the Bayon): lichen-covered head of Lokesvara.

15. Angkor Thom (the Bayon): a boat, detail from the frieze of
bas-reliefs.

16. Angkor Thom (the Bayon): soldiers of Jayavarman VII, detail
from the frieze of bas-reliefs.

17. Phnom Bakheng: sandstone lion seated on a pedestal of laterite.

18. Angkor Thom: terrace of the elephants, detail.

19. Ta Keo: general view.

20. Banteay Samré: receding pediments (reconstructed). The roof
is surmounted with filials.

21. Preah Khan (Angkor): the battle between nature and the
stone.

22. Preah Khan (Angkor): niches from which the original carvings have been torn; below them stands Garuda.

23. Neak Pean: the central sanctuary (reconstructed).

24. Neak Pean: a gargoyle.

25. Neak Pean: drowning merchants clamber to catch hold of the horse Balaha (reconstructed).

26. Banteay Srei: statue of Vishnu.

27. Preah Khan (Kompong Svay): a tower.

28. Beng Mealea: ruins tangled in the forest.

29. Ta Som: late sculpture of Jayavarman VII period; hurried, clumsy execution.

30. Banteay Chhmar: Lokesvara head.

31. Banteay Chhmar: detail of a bas-relief surrounded by the forest.

32. Wat Phu: *naga* terminal torn from the balustrade of a Khmer temple.

33. Kompong Kdei: ancient Khmer bridge under reconstruction; notice how the arches are built.

34. Kompong Kdei: arch of an ancient Khmer bridge.

35. Spean Thma: the base of an arch belonging to the bridge which carried the road from Angkor Thom to Champa.

36. An ancient inscription (John Keshishian).

37. Bronze Garuda, twelfth century (Courtesy of the Detroit Institute of Arts).

38. Head of a sleeping Vishnu, early twelfth century (Rijksmuseum, Amsterdam).

39. Preah Khan (Angkor): seated figures, fragment (Musée Labit, Toulouse).

40. Head of Buddha, late twelfth century (Ashmolean Museum, Oxford).

41. Pre-Angkor Bronze Vishnu, seventh century (Avery Brundage).

42. Reconstruction work at Angkor—every stone is numbered.

43. Cambodian youths reconstruct the ancient temples.

44. Shrine belonging to an ancient Khmer rest house at Angkor.

45. Scene in a Cambodian village. The banana trees, palms, and livestock seen here were the same in ancient times.

46. Cambodian landscape in the dry season; ancient inscriptions refer to dried-up watercourses.

47. Two present-day Cambodians, whose bearing vividly recalls that of their ancestors.

48. The Wat Koh Krishna (National Museum, Phnom Penh).

49. An intricately cast bronze hook from which a hammock would have been slung (Musée Guimet, Paris).

50. Angkor Thom: a *naga* head found at the Phimeanakas (Musée Guimet, Paris)

51. Banteay Srei: detail from a pediment (Musée Guimet, Paris).

52. An eleventh-century Sanskrit inscription which relates the foundation of a linga (Musée Guimet, Paris).

53. Statue-portrait of Jayavarman VII (National Museum, Phnom Penh).

54. Present-day Buddhist monks at Banteay Srei, a temple dedicated to the linga.

55. Angkor Thom in 1890—an artist's impression (after Fournereau).

56. The Delaporte mission at Angkor in 1873—an artist's impression (after Delaporte).

57. Wrestlers, Koh Ker style (National Museum, Phnom Penh).

58. Cambodian ballet dancers (Information Khmère, Phnom Penh).

59. An undershot waterwheel on the Siemreap River near Angkor.

paddy annually." The burning of rice with wood has survived as a custom in Thailand and Cambodia. During the Thai dynasty of Ayuthia a mock king attended the function and set fire to a straw umbrella for which different teams would compete. These teams were drawn from the mock king's retinue and wore either red (for Brahma) or green (for Indra). In Cambodia the remains of the burnt offering used to be given to the Buddhist monks.

Among the many festivals mentioned in the inscriptions of Preah Khan (Angkor) and Ta Prohm, a spring festival at Ta Prohm is described. It comprised a series of ceremonies leading up to a climax at the time of the full moon. There were two sacrifices, processions around the temple three times (*pradaksinas*) on two days, parading of banners and parasols, and dancing by male and female dancers. Ascetic young men practiced virtue by giving alms and displaying good conduct. A total of 619 divinities are mentioned, presumably statues, and these were probably draped with the immense quantities of cloth specially provided for the purpose. The sacrifices, which only specially appointed priests could perform, were animal and not human. A stone altar shaped like the base of a pedestal has been discovered at Prasat Svay Khal Tuk, several miles northeast of Beng Mealea. A similar stone altar was discovered at Banteay Srei, where an inscription refers to the distribution of wood for sacrificial burnings.

There were hundreds of small ceremonies which took place daily in the temples and for which cult objects have been discovered. Three bronze statuettes, four bracelets, and four bells have been unearthed at a village near the town of Takeo. All these objects were used by the priests in their ceremonial. In the inscriptions a distinction is made between insignia (e.g., earrings, bracelets, or crown) and emblems (e.g., white parasol or fan). Many of the processions took place in the open air, so it would have been possible to identify the more important priests by their insignia and to judge by their emblems the esteem in which they were held. The lighting of candles is a feature of most religions—so, also, was it with the Khmers. However, the people did not gather in the temples as they would today in a church. The priests lighted candles privately in the tiny chapels in which statues, washed with perfumed water, were placed. An inscription mentions a total of four thousand candles which had to be supplied to a temple. The Khmers had elegant candelabra for lighting purposes. Ritual candles were placed in cups of sand. A two-legged bronze cup in the shape of a blue lotus has been found near Mongkolborei. In present-day Cambodia, candles are attached to *popils,* small bronze objects shaped like *naga*-heads. These *popils* are used in many ceremonies, both Buddhist and those connected with nature spirits. In ancient times the *popil* was much bigger and its use less widespread. Sweet-smelling materials were burned in the temples. A slab for rolling and grinding such materials has been found at Prasat Komphus, fifteen miles northeast of Koh Ker.

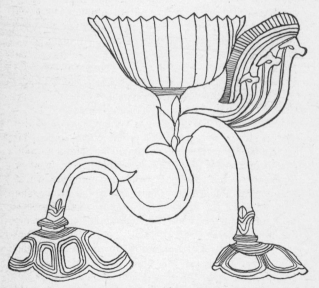

Fig. 17    Incense burner, after a bronze in the National Museum, Phnom Penh, Cambodia *(Mavis Cameron).*

Sometimes the king himself took part in religious festivals. When Chou Ta-Kouan visited Angkor, the king used to make a ceremonial visit to a small tower where there was a gold statue of Buddha. The Chinese visitor's description of the procession is a classic eyewitness account of life at Angkor. We should note in passing that the kings did not exclude themselves from rigorous religious practices. Their subjects expected them to practice meditation for long hours and thus prepare themselves for greater altruistic efforts on behalf of the Khmer kingdom. Festivals in which the king participated were holidays for the population of Angkor.

Chou Ta-Kouan describes one of the processions in which the king took part:

When the king goes out, troops lead the escort; then come the standards, military colors and music. Palace maidens, three to five hundred in number, in floral patterned fabrics, with flowers in their chignons, hold flares in their hands, and form a troop by themselves; even in plain daylight their flares are lit. Then come palace maidens carrying the royal utensils of gold and silver and a whole series of ornaments, all of a very particular kind and whose purpose is unknown to me. Then come palace maidens holding lance and buckler, who are the private guard of the palace; they also form a troop by themselves. Next come some goat carts and horse carts, all decorated in gold. The ministers, the princes are all riding elephants; in front of them [?] one sees from afar their red parasols, which are innumerable. After them arrive the wives and concubines of the king, by palanquin, cart, on horseback or elephant; they have certainly more than a hundred parasols flecked with gold. Then behind them comes the king, standing on an elephant and holding in his hand the precious sword. The elephant's tusks are also in a sheath of gold. There are more than twenty white parasols flecked [?] with gold and whose handles are of gold. Many elephants press all about him and again there are troops to protect him.[13]

[13] Chou Ta-Kouan, pp. 34–35.

Just as handfuls of rice had to be burned at the right time of year in remote provincial temples, so the prestige of the devaraja had to be maintained at Angkor itself. Single candles might be lighted at distant rest houses along the ancient Khmer roads, and thousands might be burned at Angkor. There was panoply and theatricality in Khmer festivals. The rules of religious pomp had to be obeyed. The civilization of Angkor flourished as long as the Khmers continued to believe that ostentation was compatible with true religion.

## LAW AND JUSTICE

The king had all legal power vested in himself. Whether or not he was subject to a higher religious law is not clear. The language of Khmer inscriptions suggests that the kings of Angkor were incapable of transgressing religious laws. There is a further probability that the kings, themselves gods in their own and in their subjects' estimation, did not recognize any religious law higher than their own commands. Yasovarman I was said to have been closed to evil—an idea of blamelessness which the Khmer people accepted, even though palace revolutions at Angkor proved that the opposite was true. In order to bolster their *de facto* positions of power, certain Khmer kings—Suryavarman I, for example—exacted an oath of allegiance from their captains of militia. Inscriptions record verbatim the series of promises which made up this oath. Significantly, the language used was Khmer, for the captains of militia, on whose support the king's military strength depended, were not priests. They did not know how to compose Sanskrit poems and make plays on Sanskrit words. The words of the oath were simple and revealing. The militia captains could be under no delusions about their commitments.

WE—so they swore—WILL NOT REVERE ANOTHER
KING, we shall not be enemies [of our king] and we
will not seek to harm him in any way. All actions
which are the fruit of our devotion to His Majesty we
will strive to perform them. If there is a war, we will
strive to fight and disregard life, with all our soul, in
devotion to the king. We shall not run away out of the
battle. If, in default of war, we die by suicide or sudden
death, may we obtain the recompense of people devoted
to their master.[14] If our existence remains at the service
of His Majesty up to our death, we will perform [our
duty] with devotion [to the king], whatever may be
the time and circumstances of death. If there is a
matter of service for which His Majesty orders us to
go far away, to obtain information on this matter, we
will try to get to know the thing in detail and each to
keep this promise in whatever concerns us. If all of
us who are here in person do not keep this promise
with regard to His Majesty . . . we ask that he inflict
on us royal punishments of every kind.[15] If we hide
ourselves in order not to keep this promise strictly,
may we he reborn in the thirty-two hells as long as
there shall be sun and moon.[16]

There could hardly be a more blunt statement than this.
Some remarks follow in which those obedient to the promises are guaranteed subsistence for their families provided
they also help maintain the temples. The final, but unspecified, reward will be granted to "people devoted to their
master from this world to the next world." The royal pun-

[14] In an alternative translation (see *Inscriptions du Cambodge,*
Vol. III, p. 209), Coedès rejects the idea of suddenness in favor of
"illness." The captains did not commit suicide.

[15] Instead of "he," Coedès suggests an alternative translation:
"the sovereigns who will reign in the future." Punishment by future
kings means that a man's family will be punished from one generation to the next if he betrays the king.

[16] George Coedès, "Le serment des fonctionnaires de Suryavarman I," *Bulletin de l'École Française d'Extrême-Orient,* XIII (Hanoi,
Vietnam, 1913), 15–16.

ishments to which reference is made in the oath included
the death penalty.

Rough justice was administered by the king. Inscriptions
refer to royal audiences for administering justice, and
Chou Ta-Kouan actually witnessed one. "Disputes of the
people," he writes, "however insignificant, always go to the
king." [17]

> . . . each day the king holds two audiences for affairs
> of state. There is no order of sessions. Those of the
> functionaries or the people who wish to see the king,
> sit on the ground to wait for him. At the end of some
> time, the sound of distant music is heard in the pal-
> ace; and thereupon, outside, the conches are blown as
> welcome to the king. . . . A moment later, one sees
> two palace maidens hold up the curtain with their
> slender fingers and the king, grasping the sword in his
> hand, appears standing at the golden window. Minis-
> ters and common people clasp their hands and touch
> the ground with their foreheads; when the noise of
> the conches has finished, they can hold up their
> heads. The king immediately after [?] goes to sit
> down. There where he sits, there is a lion's skin,
> which is part of the hereditary royal treasure. As
> soon as the business in hand is completed, the king
> turns around; the two palace maidens let the curtain
> fall; everybody rises. One sees by that how even in a
> kingdom of the barbarians these people do not fail to
> recognize what it is to be a king.[18]

To be a king—this was at least half the essence of the
devaraja. The other half was to be a god. Although the
Khmer king held royal audiences regularly, not every dispute came to him. A body of legal assessors and advisers
helped him by traveling to different parts of the kingdom
to hold court, and even at Angkor there were courts which

17 Chou Ta-Kouan, p. 22.
18 Ibid., p. 35.

the king did not himself attend. Within the general framework that vested all legal power in the king, something which we can call Khmer law also existed. It was not codified until long after the end of Khmer rule at Angkor. But it did exist. Like so many branches of Khmer life the law derived some, though not all, of its framework from India. Certain legal terms like case, plaintiff, proof, and sentence were borrowed from Indian terminology, and a paragraph from a well-known Hindu legal code, that of Manu, is actually reproduced verbatim in an inscription of Yasovarman I.

Khmer law consisted of a body of case law. The decisions of previous kings, recorded on palm leaves, were consulted by succeeding monarchs and their staffs. For example, an inscription of Phnom Bakheng shows that in the year of his accession (968) Jayavarman V prescribed that the edicts of his predecessor, Rajendravarman, should be registered. Clearly the king was conscious of earlier legal decisions. He did not invent the law as he went along. The five great crimes at Angkor were murder of a priest, drunkenness, theft, adultery with the wife of one's master, and being an accessory to any of these crimes. The hell scenes of Angkor Wat provide a comprehensive list of malefactors, in which are included false witnesses, madmen, thieves, incendiaries, poisoners, gluttons, adulterers, liars, and debtors. But besides these major crimes, of which the Khmers had their normal share, there were a large number of minor peccadilloes. Ordinary men and women could bring lawsuits against each other. To examine one of these in detail is to witness life in the ancient Khmer empire as it really was.

A typical case illustrating the Khmer legal process is recorded on the inscription of Tuol Rolom Tim. Although the inscription dates from the reign of Jayavarman V, it refers to events in the reign of Harshavarman II. After naming the parties in this lawsuit the inscription sets out the indictment of the plaintiffs, the rebuttal of this indictment by the defendants and the citing of additional evidence for the defense, a plea of ignorance by the plaintiffs about these statements, the magistrate's summation, and the decision of the court (two legal officials and four as-sessors) as to the punishment. In this case the plaintiffs were proved to have brought an invalid indictment and were condemned to fifty strokes on the face. Their motives in bringing up the case are obscure, and it may be that they sought to defame the defendants by casting light on earlier actions in the defendants' lives which were in some way discreditable. All this sounds rather modern. When the Khmers are seen apart from the context of their soar-ing temples and terrifying devaraja, they take on the color of ordinary people we might encounter in everyday life.

In this particular case the first party owed a buffalo to the local head of a paddy, whose duties were similar to those of an income-tax officer. To fulfill their obligation, they obtained a buffalo from the second party by deposit-ing a slave called Tai Kanhyan as part payment. So it was alleged by the plaintiffs. Already this looks like a mislead-ing and confusing case, and so it turns out. The second party contracted to supply Tai Kanhyan to a temple, from which she ran away. The first party supplied another fe-male slave as a replacement and when she also ran away, they finally sent a third slave, who happened to be the niece of the runaway Tai Kanhyan. This third slave was an obedient girl and did not run away as her aunt had done. The plaintiffs alleged that there was something in-correct in the original contract, for the slave Tai Kanhyan was only a deposit against payment and not the actual payment. The strange thing was that twenty-five years elapsed before the plaintiffs took action and brought their case. By this time the niece of Tai Kanhyan was herself a grandmother and could prove that she had worked at the temple throughout the twenty-five years. Her progeny are named on the inscription, since it was the defendants' case that the buffalo had been properly paid for in full by Tai Kanhyan's niece, who had replaced her runaway aunt. The niece, moreover, was quite a bargain; she had worked at the temple for a long time and now had children who also belonged to the temple. There was, in any event, nothing incorrect about this ancient transaction, and the plaintiffs completely failed to make a convincing case. They had simply dragged the defendants to law on a supposed technicality.

Punishments for guilty parties were severe—for example, 102 strokes with the birch for fraudulently harvesting somebody else's rice field. Besides birching, punishments included the cutting off of hands and lips and the squeezing of head and feet, which sometimes led to death. Guilty women were not exempt from these punishments, and an inscription records that a woman called Ayak had her head squeezed. A bas-relief of Banteay Chhmar shows a man with his head in the stocks, legs shackled, and chains around his middle. Chou Ta-Kouan confirms some of these punishments, such as the cutting off of hands, and relates others—burial alive for major crimes and fines for lesser crimes.

Besides trial by the king or his appointed delegates there was also a kind of trial by ordeal. This primitive form of justice was a carry-over from pre-Angkor days. An inscription refers to a man failing his oath, which means that he failed in a trial by ordeal. The kinds of ordeals which suspected persons might have to undergo are described by Chou Ta-Kouan. In the case of theft, a suspect might be required to plunge his hand into a pot of boiling water. If the skin on his hand dissolved into ribbons, he was declared guilty. If not, he was innocent. There was also another kind of ordeal, which Chou Ta-Kouan calls "celestial judgment." It probably did not take place exactly as he describes in the following passage, but this kind of ordeal did exist.

In front of the royal palace there are twelve small towers of stone. Each of the two men [accuser and accused] sits in a separate tower and is kept under watch by a member of his opponent's family. They stay one or two days, or even three or four days. When they come out, the man in the wrong never fails to have caught some illness: either he gets ulcers or catarrh or a bad fever. The man in the right does not catch anything. That is how they decide between the just and the unjust.[19]

[19] *Ibid.*, p. 23.

## BUILDING MATERIALS AND METHODS

From the earliest times wood was the chief building material of the Khmers and it was only gradually replaced by more durable substances. Even when stone began to be used, the sculptors carved as though they were using wood. In architecture wood survived suprisingly as the adjunct of stone. A richly decorated fragment of a ceiling made from a robust wood which the Cambodians call *koki* has been found at Angkor Wat. This fragment is decorated with a large eight-petaled lotus flower surrounded by four smaller-petaled lotuses. It gives striking evidence that the Khmers were master carpenters and wood-carvers.

Many examples could be cited of the use of wood in Khmer sandstone temples. Wood was used vertically to give rigidity to certain walls of Beng Mealea. In a Khmer ruin nine miles north of Pursat some drums of a column have been discovered, two of which are mortised for fitting a wooden beam. The Khmers did not as a rule employ circular columns because they resembled trees. Rare examples are found at the Baphuon (Angkor) and in a minor edifice of Preah Khan (Angkor). There was an ancient belief, still current in Cambodia, that trees could not be cut down before permission had been sought from the spirits of the forest. Even circular columns of stone were avoided because they resembled the shape of trees too closely. The spirits might remain in circular columns or enter them after they were placed in position. If spirits were present, the building might be struck by lightning or collapse in a high wind. Most Khmer pillars, consequently, were square or rectangular. The occasional use of circular columns at Angkor derived from an inversion of this superstition—a desire to bring the spirits into the building and thus conquer them.

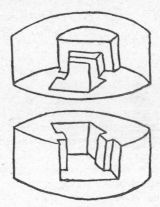

Fig. 18 Sections of a stone column mortised for fitting a wooden beam *(Mavis Cameron).*

Wooden beams and joists were frequently employed by Khmer builders. Sometimes the use of wood was illogical. For example, at Phnom Chisor (near Phnom Penh) and at Prasat Thom (Koh Ker) wood was used to reinforce entrance gateway lintels. In both places the wood has decayed, but whereas the gateway of Prasat Thom has collapsed, that of Phnom Chisor has lasted. In other words, the fortuitously practical design of Phnom Chisor could support the gateway and did not really need the wooden reinforcement, but the less practical design of Koh Ker required extra support. The Khmers did not know how to build an arch. The vaults which cover the galleries of Angkor Wat are little more than the extension of two walls upward until they meet. There is a tendency in this kind of vault for the walls to bulge and wobble. Wood was used in an incredible fashion to help hold such vaults upright. The Khmers were bad architects, but the overall design of their temples silences our criticisms.

During the Funanese period, the early inhabitants of Indochina began to use brick as well as wood. The Khmers of the pre-Angkor period relied mostly on wood, but when they wanted more durable materials, they built in brick, with some sandstone additions, and brick continued to be used at Angkor, too. Bricks in Khmer buildings are usually of good quality, well-baked, and hard. They were held together by cement made from vegetable juices, powdered limestone and palm-tree sugar. Even today bricks in ruined towers cling together by virtue of this original cementing substance and form great monoliths of masonry. Since there are so many undated sites where brick has been used, it is impossible to say whether the Khmers ever abandoned the use of brick altogether.

Brick does not seem to be a promising material for the sculptor; yet the Khmers used it and in the tenth century, especially, produced some good reliefs. The figures of Lakshmi and Vishnu on the walls of Prasat Kravanh at Angkor are successful in spite of the many vertical and horizontal lines formed by the layers of brick. In the Baksei Chamkrong at Angkor, also tenth century, laterite and sandstone and brick are used in ascending order. Another building of this period, the East Mebon, reveals a large number of small holes on the outer surface of its brickwork. An inscription says that certain sanctuaries, which can be identified with the towers of the East Mebon, were covered with stucco. The purpose of the holes was to help bind the stucco to the bricks. On some towers the outline which these stucco additions would take was first roughed out on the brick. In the eleventh century, brick remained an important material. At Phnom Chisor, for example, builders used it in quantity, even though there was a sandstone quarry on the southwest of the hill which could have supplied their needs. The Khmers had by this time mastered the use of sandstone, but they felt no pressing need to dispense with brick. Conversely, the central sanctuaries of some earlier temples—Phnom Bakheng and Phnom Krom, for example—were made entirely of sandstone, and brick was relegated to the annex edifices. Brick towers, enveloped by trees and shrubs and creepers, are a common sight in the Cambodian forest.

We should remember that rock oxidation in their rice fields was a constant threat which the Khmers had to combat. Nevertheless, the laterite produced by this process proved to be a useful building material. Although it looks porous, with its many small cavities, it does, in fact, resist rising moisture well and is an excellent material for walls or foundations (see Plate 17). Some laterite is almost black, but usually it is red and resembles brick from a distance. Like brick, laterite is not a suitable material for sculpture, but the Khmers did occasionally use it for this purpose. Two small laterite lions were discovered in Takeo province. Broken chips of laterite were sometimes used to form a base on which a temple would be built. Where deep holes had to be filled, charcoal made from burned wood was used as an additional foundation material. Two layers of laterite blocks would be placed on the rubble base, then a slab of sandstone at ground level. The exterior of a temple usually consisted of carved sandstone blocks backed by blocks of laterite. Earth was also used for foundations. More than three feet of earth was piled up around Ta Prohm, and about eight feet around the Phimeanakas. Laterite can be quite soft when it is cut from the ground, but it hardens quickly in the sun. When Jayavarman VII built Angkor Thom, a moat was dug and the laterite which came from the trench was used to build the walls of the city.

The Khmers also employed metal bolts in their building and sculpture. Double T-shaped iron crampons were used to hold blocks of sandstone together. The marks where these crampons were fixed can be seen at Angkor even though new bolts have been placed in the original holes. An iron bolt for fixing the balustrades of window spaces has been found at Preah Thkol (part of Preah Khan at Kompong Svay), and a statue with T-marks at the elbows, where metal joints were used to fix or repair the lower parts of the arms, has been found near the east gate of Angkor Thom. Metal claws were also used to clamp blocks of sandstone while they were lifted. Some of these blocks look as if they had been bitten by the claws.

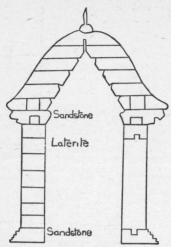

Fig. 19    Laterite
and sandstone sand-
wiched together. The
diagram also shows
how the Khmers
built their arches
*(Mavis Cameron)*.

We must now consider the main building material used
by the Khmers—sandstone. The Khmers' skill in carpentry
greatly influenced their handling of sandstone. At Ashram
Maharosei, a pre-Angkor temple, one stone block appears
to have been sawed as though it were a piece of wood;
only a saw could have produced such a regular joint.
Sandstone became the Khmers' substitute for wood. Sometimes, as at Chau Say Tevoda (north gopura, east face),
the sandstone outer wall of a temple was carved away to
almost nothing. Some of this sandstone "marquetry" is so
thin that cement has had to be added on the inside surface
to hold it together. The Khmers were able to use patterns
learned from wood-carving because their sandstone was
comparatively soft. This softness was caused by the presence of decomposed feldspars, micas, and cement in the

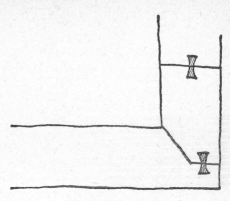

Fig. 20 Diagram to illustrate the use of iron crampons with which to hold the sandstone together *(Mavis Cameron)*.

stone. Tools for working such stone did not have to be particularly sharp.

There are three main types of sandstone in ancient Khmer monuments—the greenish sandstone from which parts of many temples at Angkor are built (e.g., Angkor Wat, Ta Prohm, Pré Rup), a slightly different kind found in the temple of Ta Keo, and the reddish sandstone from which Banteay Srei is constructed. The resistance of Cambodian sandstone is extremely variable, and may be anything from one to four and a half tons per square inch. Surprisingly enough, the sandstone is not particularly porous.

Sandstone was plentiful in Cambodia, but the quarries were inconveniently situated. Phnom Kulen, twenty-five miles from Angkor, was a good source. The greenish-looking stone, used for so many buildings at Angkor, can still be obtained from an old working at Trapeang Thma Dap, and the reddish stone, used for Banteay Srei, is available from Phon Preah Put. Defunct workings on the south side of a low-lying spur in a region known locally as Phnom

Bei can be reached by an hour's walk from Beng Mealea. The Khmers did not have to sink pit shafts or galleries, since the sandstone protrudes from the surface and makes open-cast working a simple matter. Gaps have been discovered in the sandstone face, the shape of which indicates the blocks of stone have been removed by human intervention. A combination of crowbars, bare hands, and fire was needed to break stone from the quarry. Crowbars were used to drill gutters around likely blocks and expose them. Crews of workers placed their hands on these blocks and tried to break them off by brute force. Fires were lighted around the bedrock in attempts to split them. Each stone had to be specially prepared, but this was not done on the quarry site.

The size of the sandstone blocks varied considerably; some were gigantic monoliths. There is one such monolith at the opening of the bay leading to the towers of the Bakong, its estimated size being 106 cubic feet and its weight almost seven tons. A monolith used for a large *naga* at Preah Vihear weighed nine and three-quarter tons. Most of the sandstone blocks were much smaller than this, but transporting them from the quarry to the building site was still a problem. There were two ways to bring sandstone from Phnom Kulen to Angkor. The Siemreap River, which rose in the Phnom Kulen hills, provided a direct means of communication with Angkor, where the network of canals could be used to bring sandstone barges and rafts to the required site. When quarries were situated far from the Siemreap River, a route lay open by way of the O Samrong to Kompong Kleang, then down the Stung Kompong Cham to the Great Lake. Craft using this route entered the Siemreap River where it flowed into the Great Lake, and went upstream to Angkor.

Land transport also played an important part. Hill-bound temples, such as Banteay Chhmar and Preah Vihear, could not be supplied by water. In fact, at Preah Vihear the hillside quarries were close to the building site, and the sandstone blocks did not have to be transported from a distance. Oxcarts would have been too feeble for carrying stone, since their wooden axles break easily in rough country. Elephants did not have sufficient stamina to haul stone

Fig. 21   Khmers moving stone by water *(Mavis Cameron).*

overland from the quarries, though they were used for
moving stone short distances on the building sites themselves. For overland transport, human power was used. A
bas-relief of the Bayon shows human beings pulling a
block of stone with ropes and easing its progress with a
crowbar. Twenty-five men would have been needed to
move blocks weighing two or three tons. The *naga*-mono-
lith of Preah Vihear is pitted with some sixty small holes.
A hundred and sixty men would have been required to
pull it up the hill by ropes secured to sixty pegs placed in
the holes. Where dates are ascribed to Khmer temples,
these are the dates of dedication taken from the inscriptions. The inscriptions do not say how long it took to build
each temple, but probably the most time-consuming operation was transporting the stone from the quarry.

The dressing of sandstone took place on the building
site, and one interpretation of a bas-relief of the Bayon
shows how this was done with a team of at least four men.
Some scaffolding was erected, consisting of two vertical
trestles and a horizontal crossbar between them. One man
crouched on the crossbar and supervised a sling that was
buckled to the bar. One or more persons operated a lever

which interlocked with a yoke pegged onto the upper side
of a sandstone block. The sling through which the lever
passed was made of rattan bands wound together. Since it
probably grew hot with friction, the man on the horizontal
crossbar had to keep the sling moist. The yoke consisted of
pegs, a harness, and a loop. So that this yoke could be attached firmly to the upper side of the stone, four or six
holes were dug in the surface to receive the wooden pegs.
The harness, made of rattan bands, was attached to these
pegs. The loop, through which the lever passed, was fastened to the middle of the harness. When the men operat-
ing the lever depressed their end, the other end engaged the
loop and lifted the stone off the ground.

The dressing process could now begin. Two more men,
using wooden poles, pushed the sandstone block to and
fro. This movement caused the lower surface of the
raised block to chafe against the upper surface of another
block placed underneath it. Thus, the rough edges of both
blocks were smoothed by contact, and the two blocks
would eventually become close-fitting bedfellows in the
fabric of a temple. The joints often did not run at right
angles, but they were still close-fitting. In parts of Angkor
Wat the shape of each stone is determined arbitrarily by
the shape of the previous stone. Besides the dressing of top
and bottom surfaces, the sides of each stone were also
dressed where they would touch. After the wooden pegs
that held the yoke in place were removed, the holes were
filled with a mixture of lime and gravel. Sandstone pegs
were sometimes used, in which case they were broken off
*in situ* when the dressing process was complete. A stone
peg used on a block of Banteay Srei split the stone.
Wooden pegs were preferable.

Although the Khmers used painstaking care to make
their sandstone blocks fit together, they did not lay them
in logical fashion. The towers of the Bayon provide a classic example of bad workmanship. Instead of staggering
successive layers of stones in the towers, the Khmers piled
up the blocks regularly. When Angkor was abandoned,
these towers fell apart at the seams, along which the roots
of the silk-cotton tree made unimpeded progress. Towers
of stones piled up in this even layer-cake fashion toppled

and crashed to the ground. Such inadequacy is surprising because the Khmers have a good eye in architectural matters. The southwest corner of the Angkor Thom wall is only two degrees more than a right angle, and the northwest corner only two and a half degrees less.

When the dressing of the sandstone was completed, the next job was to raise the blocks to the great heights where the towers of a temple might be under construction. The actual carving was not done on the ground. The stones had to be put in their final resting place and allowed to dry out before the sculptor started his work. Bamboo scaffolding was erected to provide the workmen with a foothold and to raise the sandstone. The Khmers used winches and pulleys to haul up the blocks. A bas-relief of the Bayon shows a vessel, in the stern of which a sailor is maneuvering an anchor in the water. This anchor is tied to a hawser which passes over a winch. Building pulleys and winches are not illustrated on the Bayon reliefs, but the Khmers knew the principles involved. When the first and second recesses of a temple were completed, holes were drilled in the flagstones and new scaffolding secured, enabling the builders to go higher and higher. These holes were also used for securing temporary wooden structures on stilts into which the workmen crept to escape the sun at midday and in which they stored their tools. The sight of Cambodian workmen crouching on the ruined temples under makeshift shelters of wood and palm leaves gives us some idea of what it must have been like on the construction sites. The Bakong, for example, is thoroughly exposed to the sun and becomes a sweltering inferno during the hottest part of the day.

We have said that the Khmers did not distinguish between sculptors and architects. The work of both represented equal devotion to a religious ideal. When at last the sequence of quarrying, transporting, dressing, and raising the sandstone was completed, the moment for carving had arrived. Khmer tools were extremely simple. They consisted of a mallet such as we might use to knock in a tent peg, a knife, and a chisel. Mallets are depicted in the hell scene of the Angkor Wat frieze, and an actual wooden mallet was discovered at Ta Prohm. The delicate molding

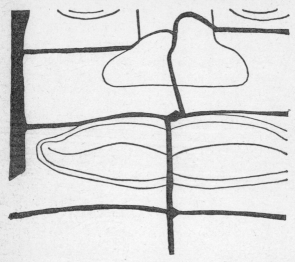

Fig. 22   Angkor Thom (the Bayon): Lokesvara face; note how the stones have been placed *(Mavis Cameron)*.

and intricate designs which the Khmers carved—mostly on the outside walls of their chapels and towers—are themselves a triumph. Unfinished carvings show how the Khmers built up the most complicated designs from simple floral motifs and geometrical forms. A basic shape such as the flowering lotus could be elaborated so that it looked like a priceless brooch or medallion. Drooping scrolls, dolphinlike swirls, interlaced S-motifs, and birds or animals springing from complicated lotus buds make some of the carvings seem baroque. Some of the neatest and yet most intricate designs occur on the false doors which were a feature of Khmer architecture. Lintels, too, show brilliance in the execution of minute detail. Yet, as with bas-reliefs, the Khmers did not let these multitudinous decorations detract from the overall design. In all Khmer architecture there was only one building which might be called baroque—the Bayon. The rest reflected the discipline and order which were hallmarks of a successful devaraja and a flourishing empire.

Fig. 23   Angkor Wat: detail of decorative motifs on the west gopura (*Mavis Cameron*).

## ENTERTAINMENT

The farmer-builder-soldiers on whose work the Khmer empire depended were not above enjoying themselves. Dancing to the sound of drums took place in the remotest villages. One of the most haunting sounds in Cambodia is

the music of a marriage feast or of a monastery festival
pealing through the forest or across the rice fields. Both
the ancient inscriptions and the bas-reliefs indicate that
sounds of a similar kind haunted the court and temples of
Angkor. No actual music has survived, but we know what
instruments were used. Percussion (drums, gongs, cym-
bals, tambourines, and bells) enlivened the royal processions. Stringed instruments (bamboo guitars and harps)
were used for more intimate occasions, as background for
the reading aloud of the holy books or as an accompani-
ment for the king's dancers. Wind instruments (conches
and trombones with conchlike ends) were used to an-
nounce the presence of the devaraja. Two types of harps,
angular and rounded, have been noted on the bas-reliefs.
These originated in India, where the harp died out as early
as the sixth century and was replaced by the lute as principal instrument. At Angkor, the harp continued to be used
during the period of Khmer greatness and was eventually
replaced by sets of gongs slung from a pole. The significant fact about both harp and gongs is that they produce
fixed sounds. From this we may surmise that the Khmers
used a musical scale of seven equal tones. Traditionally,
according to the ancients, this scale was used by musicians
who accompanied the celestial dancers in their steps.
Many such dancers were depicted in Khmer sculpture.

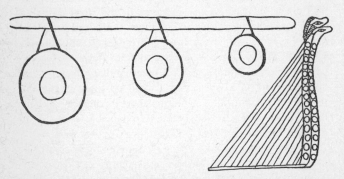

Fig. 24   Khmer musical instruments: two "fixed-sound" instruments,
the harp and gongs (Mavis Cameron).

Sometimes the king held a public entertainment in the open space at the center of Angkor Thom. Chou Ta-Kouan attended one of these spectacles and provides an eye-witness description. "In front of the royal palace," he writes, "they assemble a stand capable of holding more than a thousand persons, and it is entirely adorned with lanterns and flowers." He then describes the building of various stands from scaffolding similar to that used for temples. "Each night"—the period of rejoicing went on for several days—"they construct three, four, five or six such stands. Rockets and firecrackers are put on top. . . . At nightfall the presence of the king is requested at the entertainment. Fireworks are let off and the firecrackers lit. The fireworks can be seen more than a hundred stades [from Angkor]. The firecrackers are as large as siege machines, and their detonation shakes the whole city." [20]

Besides this official fireworks display the Khmers had other kinds of entertainment. Elephant fights and hog fights took place in special paddocks. Cockfighting was a popular sport on which the peasants betted, but it was frowned on by the priests. The streets of Angkor Thom provided many amusements for the curious. There were snake charmers and storytellers, minstrels and dwarfs. Those who preferred the seclusion of their houses could play chess. In back streets members of the royal corporations could be seen rehearsing their skills and training. Boxers sparred with each other. Wrestlers practiced their holds. Archers trained in the use of crossbows. A bas-relief of Angkor Wat shows a Khmer archery target of a bird mounted on a wheel. Slaves held up these targets on the end of upright poles while the sharpshooters tried their luck. Yasovarman I was reputed to be able to shoot a moving bird while he was being carried in his palanquin. Team games also existed. Chou Ta-Kouan mentions a ball-game, and what might be polo is depicted on a bas-relief of the Elephant Terrace at Angkor Thom.

[20] *Ibid.*, p. 21.

Fig. 25  Angkor Wat: cockfighting, detail from bas-relief *(Mavis Cameron)*.

The warm climate and the fact that houses were built on stilts enabled the Khmers to amuse themselves out-of-doors and in public. But the common people were excluded from the most sophisticated entertainments, which the king arranged in private—the performances of ancient stories by actors, dancers, and musicians. The common people also performed these stories from the *jatakas,* but the royal troupe was the best. An inscription says that a wife of Jayavarman VII "charged her own dancing-girls to play, to give representations from the *jatakas.*" Cambodian ballet was born at Angkor (see Plate 58); the numerous figured dancers on the walls of the temples had their counterparts in real life. It is perhaps wrong to speak of these representations as "entertainment," since they were an im-

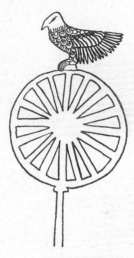

Fig. 26 Angkor
Wat: Khmer archery
target, detail from
bas-relief *(Mavis
Cameron)*.

portant part of Khmer religious life. Many of the temples
had their own troupes of dancers who enacted scenes from
the holy books at festivals. A Cambodian writer has tried
to express the Khmer heritage of his country in a play
called *The Stone Which Dances*. It tells of a Cambodian
sculptor who tried to convince the world that a stone
could dance. In Angkor Wat the stones really do dance.
Performance of the *jatakas* in the presence of a Khmer
king and queen must have been a splendid occasion.

Fig. 27  Angkor Wat: female figure, detail from bas-relief *(Mavis Cameron)*.

Their public and private amusements indicate the appealing humanity of the Khmers. The relics of their civilization are awe-inspiring, and the hold which religion exerted on them is rather terrifying. But they had a sense of humor, too. This is nowhere seen to better effect than in a bas-relief of Angkor Wat which shows a pair of monkeys dancing and beating drums in a frenzy of enjoyment.

## SOCIAL CUSTOMS

The origins of present-day Cambodian customs may not be attributed wholesale to the Khmer civilization, though some elements do derive from ancient times. Instead, we must rely chiefly on Chou Ta-Kouan for our knowledge of Khmer customs. This is unfortunate in some ways because his accounts are not well organized, and he tends to belabor the more lurid aspects of his subject. Archaeological findings expand our knowledge, however, and provide interesting sidelights of Khmer life.

An inscription says that the marriage of an official to the sister-in-law of Suryavarman I was celebrated in the presence of the sacred fire. Ma Touan-Lin, who wrote about an earlier period than Chou Ta-Kouan, said that weddings included the giving of gifts by the man, a ceremony by day and night, and the establishment of a home by the newly married pair. According to another inscription, a wedding party was sometimes held in honor of the bridegroom. The Khmers had magic diagrams which enabled them to read their horoscopes and decide what days were favorable for marriage. Khmer girls had premarital intercourse with their future husbands if they felt so inclined, and there was no disapproval of those who did. Intercourse continued normally in married life, but if a Khmer husband was away for more than ten nights, his wife would say: "I am not a spirit; how may I sleep by myself?" [21] Marriage was an established institution. If a husband caught his wife committing adultery, he might put the lover in the stocks until he was promised some recompense. Such details come from Chou Ta-Kouan, who remarks, for good measure, that Khmer girls were very passionate.

In a society such as the Khmers' the fertility of the land and of the people was closely linked. One of the desired objects produced by the churning of the Sea of Milk was the goddess of plenty. Since the Khmer empire depended on an expanding population, it was the duty of the Khmer wife to produce children, who in turn had to be fed. The Khmers believed in previous lives and rebirth, so the arrival of a baby was linked in their minds with the death of some person who had lived earlier. For reasons of health they feared, too, that a mother might lose her own life in pregnancy. A statue of a woman breast-feeding a baby has been found between Ta Keo and the East Baray, and similar figures have been discovered at the East Mebon and Baphuon. Since all these statues are decapitated, it is possible that a rite existed whereby a mother in travail could be saved if an effigy of a maternity figure was sacrificed in her place.

Once a child was born, Chou Ta-Kouan informs us, the mother made a mixture of hot rice and salt which she applied to herself. Twenty-four hours later she could resume normal life, and her figure would have contracted to its pre-pregnancy dimensions. Chou Ta-Kouan says that he saw a mother going down to the river to bathe with her baby the day after it was born. One or two days after the confinement the mother would resume intercourse with her husband. These details are more frank than any which it is possible to obtain from the Cambodians, who are extremely reticent about their sexual habits. However, in both Khmer and Cambodian society, the girls wed in their teens. The Khmers bore children in prodigious numbers, but many died in infancy. After repeated childbirth the

21 *Ibid.*, p. 17.

women at Angkor passed directly from youth to late middle age. They lost their good looks much earlier than is usual in our society.

The bas-reliefs of Banteay Chhmar give some insight into a woman's life with her children. One panel shows a Khmer woman, accompanied by three children, running with all her might to obtain rice from a central distribution point. Another shows some women handling clothes which they have just washed or dyed. If they lived at Angkor, they would bathe in pools or in the Siemreap River. Chou Ta-Kouan describes the scene just as it was:

> The country is terribly hot and one would not dream of passing a day without bathing several times. Even at nighttime one cannot miss doing it once or twice. There are no bathhouses or washbasins or buckets. But each family has a pool; if not, two or three families have one in common. When the father, mother, or elderly people are in the pool, their sons and daughters do not go in there. Or if the young people are already in the pool, the older folk stand aside from them. But if one is of the same age, one pays no attention; the women hide their sex with the left hand on entering the water, and that is all. Every three or four or five or six days the women from the city, three by three or five by five, go to bathe in the river outside the city. When they arrive at the riverbank, they take off the piece of material which covers their body and enter the water. It is by thousands that they gather at the river. Even the women of noble houses take part [in this kind of bathing] and they are not at all ashamed. . . . The water is always hot as if it was heated on the fire. . . .[22]

Knowledge of Khmer sanitation comes, once again, from Chou Ta-Kouan. He interpolates some remarks about Khmer latrines in his section on agriculture. After discussing the fact that the Khmers do not use human manure to

[22] *Ibid.,* p. 33.

fertilize their gardens and are horrified at such a—Chinese —custom, he writes:

> For two or three families, the people dig a trench which they cover with grass [?]; when it is full, they cover it and dig another one elsewhere. When they have been to the latrines, they always go into the pool to wash themselves, but only use the left hand. The right hand is kept for eating. When they see a Chinese man going to the latrines and wiping himself with paper, they make a mock of him and even want to ban him from their houses. Among the women there are some who urinate standing up. This is really absurd.[23]

The priests had entrée into the houses of the common people, where they performed a series of ceremonies, the nature of which we do not know. As a child grew he or she became used to the constant visits of priests to the house. Rules were priest-given, and family precepts came from the same source. At puberty there were special rites. We do not know what most of these rites were, but Chou Ta-Kouan, who was inquisitive about the sex life of the Khmers, describes the ceremony of *tchen-t'an*. The *tchen-t'an* ceremony was performed on girls aged seven to nine or, in poor families, when they were eleven. Neighboring families arranged to hold these ceremonies on the same night so that there might be ten taking place at the same time on the same street. They could not be performed except on the day and night appointed by the astrologers.

Such ceremonies were an excuse for a banquet and music, but regulations had to be followed. A special candle had to be obtained from the royal storehouse. A stand had to be erected, on which were placed figurines of men and animals. Two tents had to be made from rich silks— one for the young girl and one for the priest who would perform the ceremony. Friends and relatives gathered around the tents, and the candle was duly lighted. When it

[23] *Ibid.*, p. 25.

had burned to a certain point, the priest would leave his tent, enter the tent of the girl, and deflower her. The purpose of these puberty rites was to insure the continuing fertility of the people. The candle used in the *tchen-t'an* ceremony was probably quite large—like the vossa candles in Cambodia today—and represented the linga, that important Khmer palladium. The priests who performed the ceremonies were richly paid with alcohol, rice, cloth, silk, betel, and silver. Their hold over the common people appeared to be all-enveloping.

Although death was the gate to rebirth, the Khmers indulged in great lamentation when members of their family died. Persons who died without leaving an heir were especially pitied, and the king arranged for offerings to be made to their spirits from public funds. The funerary nature of the Angkor site was uppermost in the minds of the Khmers. The inscription of Preah Khan (Angkor) says that the site was possibly holier than Allahabad in India, a place highly regarded by the Hindus for incinerations and bathing of ashes. Hell—an intermediate state between death and reincarnation—was depicted in lavish detail on the frieze of Angkor Wat. The Khmers did not limit themselves to any one way of burying their dead. Corpses could be wrapped in mats and exposed outside the city. (A bas-relief of Banteay Chhmar shows vultures waiting to spring on dead bodies.) Or, the dead could be placed in coffins. The Cambodians place corpses in a crouching position when putting them in coffins, and the stone sarcophagi of the Khmers were large enough to receive corpses laid out in this way. Most of these sarcophagi had a hole through which liquid from the dead body could drain away. Later, the bodies may have been removed from the coffins and cremated. Some terraces in the center of Angkor Thom look as though they could have been used as the base for cremation pyres, and Chou Ta-Kouan says that cremation was being gradually introduced when he visited the region.

## PLACE OF WOMEN

We have touched on the domestic life of Khmer women and have seen them with their children. We must now examine the place of women in the Khmer world. There were two distinct classes of women at Angkor—commoners and nobility. The women of noble birth intermarried with the kings and priests. Parasols and shaded palanquins protected them from the sun, giving them a pallid complexion—"white as jade," Chou Ta-Kouan described it. The women who helped the Chinese in the market with business transactions were swarthy. The difference in pigmentation between the two classes was, however, only one of degree. Basically, all Khmer women had burnished brown skin. The common people were very dark, sometimes nearly black-brown, and the noble ladies a lighter color. Both classes of women occupied a dominant place in Khmer life, but the influence of upper-class women was marked. Usurpers of the Khmer throne had to show their relationship to previous kings through intermarriage. In priestly families descent and inheritance followed the female line. An inscription shows that a family connected with Prasat Kok Po at Angkor procured posts for the men who married into it simply because of their wives' position and succession.

The noble women usually stayed out of sight at Angkor. They spent their time in intellectual pursuits and led a sophisticated feministic existence. Inscriptions mention certain Khmer queens by name, and even allowing for flattery, the women of the Khmer court emerge as personalities who rivaled the devaraja himself. Tilaka, the mother of the young priest who attended the colloquium of Jayavarman VI, was reputed to have great intelligence and knowledge. It was predicted that she would marry a Sivaite who, "as the end of the hot season scatters the clouds, so he propagates Sivaite dogmas." Tilaka's maternal uncle invited this man to a party which took place in a pavilion decorated with flowers where Tilaka's father was "surrounded by a crowd of his relatives tasting the pleasures of the situation." [24] Another lady of rank, the mother of Jayavarman VII, is described as occupying a position at court, observing the rules of Buddhism, and showing favor to those practicing Buddhist rules.

The two successive wives of Jayavarman VII filled revealing posts of importance at Angkor. Jayarajadevi, the king's first wife, is said to have "taken as her own daughters, hundreds of miserable young girls abandoned by their mothers" and to have resettled them.[25] She was instructed in Buddhism by her elder sister, Indradevi, and apparently learned some magic way to conjure up the image of her husband, who spent a period of his reign fighting a war in Champa. When he returned from the wars, she loaded him with gifts. When Jayarajadevi died, the king married Indradevi, who was—according to inscription—"intelligent by nature, scholarly, very pure, devoted to her husband." She held the post of lecturer in a Buddhist monastery (an unusual position for a woman to have), and was even "named chief teacher by the king."

In an age when flower arrangement and cosmetics occupy the interest and leisure of so many women, it is pleasant to look back at an ancient society where the same interests existed. The extraordinary hairstyles of the *apsarases* at Angkor Wat reflect the interest of the Khmer ladies themselves (see Plate 8). Cambodian perfume, *tuk ap,* also existed at Angkor. One of its chief components is styrax, which the Khmers obtained from north Indochina. The styrax tree grows to a height of twenty to thirty feet, and its sap is allowed to run from a gash in the trunk for about two

24 Louis Finot, "L'inscription de Ban Theat," *Bulletin de l'École Française d'Extrême-Orient,* XII (Hanoi, Vietnam, 1912), 24.
25 George Coedès, ed., *Inscriptions du Cambodge,* Vol. II (Hanoi, Vietnam, 1942), 178.

months. Yellow globules are then harvested and used for making perfume. Other ingredients were dried flowers, yellow cane sugar, and santal. The flowers were boiled, and the mixture infused with smoke from burning santal and styrax. Khmer women also used musk.

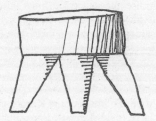

Fig. 28   Stone on which perfumes were beaten out (*Mavis Cameron*).

According to an eleventh-century inscription, a woman called Madhyadesa held the post of florist "because of her beauty and her intelligence among women." She worked at the royal palace. Khmer ladies of rank were inseparable from the flowers they used to adorn themselves and the royal apartments. As the lotus grows in pools throughout Cambodia, so the lotus motif springs up throughout Khmer art, architecture, and literature. In Khmer sculpture the lotus signifies water, but it also represents the earth spread on the surface of the waters. The lotus motif on the central tower of Banteay Samré is almost nine feet high, and an earring on a statue of Preah Pithu (Angkor) is composed of six lotuses in various stages of growth. Some of the lotuses in Khmer art resemble stylized intestines wandering through some bizarre digestive system. The Khmer ladies delighted in these myriad shapes and curves, and literary references to them are extravagant. An eye, for instance, is referred to as a mass of red and blue

lotuses, and the Khmer king is said to be like the moon,
the enemy of lotuses—presumably because lotuses close
their petals at nighttime.

A bas-relief of the Bayon shows a Khmer lady of rank,
who may be the royal florist, picking a lotus from the
water. Picking a flower is one of the actions which Cambodian ballet dancers mime to perfection. The girls who
dance in this ballet are the spiritual inheritors of a dance
technique which also pleased the Khmer kings at Angkor.
The audience at the Cambodian ballet does not watch to
find out what is going to happen, but to confirm that simple
actions like the picking of a flower are the same as they have
always been. If the Cambodian kings of the past did not like
the way in which a flower was picked, they would stop the
performance and order the dancing mistress to replay the
scene as it should be. To imagine the Khmer court as a place
filled with scholarly, pale-skinned, lotus-picking and lotus-
arranging ladies sounds fanciful, but it is near the truth. Sir
Osbert Sitwell misunderstood the towers of Angkor Wat
when he wrote that they were like wings. They are lotus
buds—and to us a constant reminder of the flower which
permeated the Khmer civilization and so delighted its powerful female members (see Plate 2).

## MEANS OF TRAVEL

The Khmers were able road builders, but their roads did
not go far into the recesses of the Khmer empire. There
was a road to Champa, but no road to Vientiane or
Nghean. When the Khmers ventured into the hills in
search of tribesmen who would make good slaves, they
used paths and jungle tracks. Some Khmer roads have
been metaled in recent times, and they still provide the
most direct routes for crossing Cambodia. Others are off

the beaten track. In addition to the minor roads running
from Angkor to Banteay Chhmar and from Beng Mealea
to Koh Ker, there were three major roads from Angkor:
one leading northwest and two running east. These roads
usually ran on raised laterite or on earth causeways and
can be identified standing above the surrounding plain.
Ancient ruins of bridges and rest houses, have been found
dotted along them.

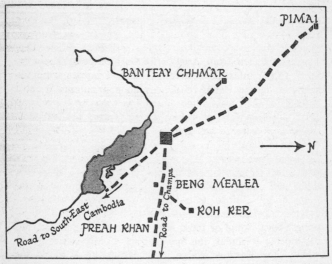

Fig. 29   The ancient Khmer network of roads centered on Angkor
(*John Stafford*).

The northwest road ran from Angkor to Pimai through
the Dangrek hills. It linked the general area of Mahidharapura with Angkor and had been in use for most of the
twelfth century. The inscription of Preah Khan (Angkor)
says that there were seventeen rest houses on this road.
Some were made of wood and have disappeared. Along
the first section of the northwest road there are ruins of

three rest houses, but within a comparable distance of Pimai the remains of only one have been found.

An east road leading from Angkor Thom to Beng Mealea, and from there to Preah Khan of Kompong Svay, continued all the way to the capital of Champa. It was left unfinished, however. Either of the two Cham capitals, Vijaya (Binh-Dinh) or Panduranga (Phan-Rang), could have been intended as the terminus of this road. The inscription of Preah Khan (Angkor) says that there were fifty-seven rest houses on a road to the east. Intermediate rest houses have been discovered at Beng Mealea and at Preah Khan of Kompong Svay, but none has been found farther east than Preah Khan of Kompong Svay. Another road to the east, that on which the inscription of Preah Khan (Angkor) says there were forty-four rest houses, has been traced from Angkor to the Kompong Thom region. If the intervals between these rest houses were the same as on the Pimai road, we can assume that it must have run for at least some 342 miles. Like the other road to the east, it was not finished, and its final destination is not even known. It was not long enough to reach the capitals of Champa.

The second road to the east is today the most accessible of ancient Khmer roads. It has been metaled in recent times and carries the main road from Siemreap to Kompong Thom. Before its modernization there were twenty-two ancient Khmer bridges between Angkor and Kompong Thom. Some of these have had to be dismantled, but the most spectacular, the Spean Praptos, still carries heavy traffic. The Praptos bridge, near Kompong Kdei, is the largest Khmer bridge in existence, and its twenty-one arches carry the road over a deep ravine (see Plate 33). The river flowing beneath is the Stung Chikreng, which also bisects the other road to the east between Angkor and Preah Khan of Kompong Svay. There is another impressive bridge here, the Spean Ta Ong, second only to the Spean Praptos. Khmer bridges display again the Khmers' inability to build a proper arch. Stones are piled up in heaps until they meet at the top in a leaning fashion (see Plate 34).

Bridges were built of laterite, but they often had sand-

stone additions of balustrades with the familiar *naga*-heads
at each end. On some sites these serpents' heads peer pro-
vocatively from the bushes and indicate the presence of an
ancient bridge. The streams have changed their course in
some regions, so that today the ancient bridges stand high
and dry. This is true of the impressive Spean Thma bridge
at Angkor (see Plate 35). It lies east of the Thommanon
and once carried the road to Champa across the Siemreap
River. The present course of the river digs much deeper
into the surface of the ground than did its old course
under the Spean Thma.

Khmer roads were not safe places to travel unescorted.
Besides the danger of pirates, there was the risk of meet-
ing gall hunters from Champa or from Angkor. The purpose of the gall harvest was to collect human gall and use
it to promote courage in animals, especially in elephants.
A nineteenth-century traveler in Cambodia reported that
the custom still existed at that time. Chou Ta-Kouan describes it, saying that it was instigated by the king of
Champa but had been discontinued by the end of the thirteenth century. It is more than likely that the Khmers also
indulged in this custom. "At nighttime," writes Chou Ta-
Kouan, "men were posted in many regions in the busiest
localities of towns and villages" and on the main roads. "If
they met people who were out at night, they covered their
heads with a hood fastened with a cord, and with a little
knife removed the gall at the base of the right side. They
waited until they had the right amount of gall, then
offered it to the king of Champa. One year it happened
that they took a Chinese man's gall and put it with the
rest, but subequently all the gall in the jar went bad and
they could not use it." [26] This last remark of Chou Ta-
Kouan suggests that he tried to make the Khmers refrain
from collecting Chinese gall. If the Khmers or Chams
could be persuaded that the gall of a Chinese person
would make the rest go bad, then Chou Ta-Kouan and his
compatriots could travel at night with impunity.

Since it was inadvisable to travel at night, rest houses
were established at frequent intervals along the roads.

26 Chou Ta-Kouan, pp. 32–33.

They also provided places where travelers could rest during the heat of the day. The Cambodian equivalent, the wooden *sala,* is a blessing to the traveler who needs to be protected from the sun at midday. Jayavarman VII built many rest houses on the roads, but the idea of the rest house was not his exclusively. In the ninth century, parts of the hermitages established by Yasovarman I were set apart as staging points for travelers. Also, the SKT inscription says of the priest who caused it to be written: "Wholly devoted to the good of others, he made houses and temples along the roads to favor caravans of travelers." Chou Ta-Kouan was impressed by the rest houses, which he said were like stage posts along the great roads of China.

The actual sleeping and eating quarters of the rest houses were made of wood and have perished. But each rest house had a chapel, and where these chapels were made of sandstone, their ruins have survived (see Plate 44). They consisted of a tower on a rectangular base, a long room, and a porch. The inscription of Preah Khan (Angkor) mentions that the rest house there contained a statue. A pool has been discovered southeast of the Teap Chei rest house, east of Beng Mealea. Clearly, the provision of shelter and food to travelers was regarded as a religious duty which the king took most seriously. In the time of Jayavarman VII there were 121 rest houses altogether: fifty-seven on the road to Champa, seventeen on the road to Pimai, and forty-four on the other east road. Three additional rest houses existed at undetermined sites.

The normal way of traveling along these ancient roads was to walk. Elephants, oxcarts, palanquins, horses, and, in the rainy season, boats were also used. Elephants, frequently depicted on the bas-reliefs, were an important feature of the Khmer army when it moved along the road to Champa. Oxcarts were also important, especially for carrying baggage and food. Fragments of an oxcart carved in sandstone were discovered under the root of a tree at the northwest Prasat Chrung of Angkor Thom. A typical oxcart is shown on the bas-reliefs of Banteay Chhmar. Although Cambodian oxcarts are the same as the Khmers' and creak and lurch and break down, they are a good means of transport. Their large wooden wheels enable them to go through almost anything, and deep mud presents no problem to them.

The ladies of the Khmer court traveled in palanquins. These litters, depicted frequently on the bas-reliefs, consisted of a hammock slung from a W-shaped pole and shaded by an elaborately carved roof. An inscription mentions that Suryavarman I gave an official a gift of a palanquin decorated with serpents' heads and adorned with gold stars on its pole. An intricately cast bronze hook from which the hammock would have been slung is on display at the Musée Guimet in Paris (see Plate 49).

Horses were also used as a means of transport, especially in the hills. According to Chou Ta-Kouan, the horses were very small. The same is true of Cambodian horses today. Despite their size, however, they are surprisingly tough. Unlike horses from more temperate climates they can withstand great heat. They can also ford rapids and trot happily in dense jungle where tigers may be waiting to spring. The Khmers did not operate in the hills of Indochina if they could avoid it. In the plain they preferred to use elephants rather than horses.

Fig. 30   Baphuon: horses, detail from bas-relief of the west gopura (*Mavis Cameron*).

## HEALTH MEASURES

The keynotes of Jayavarman VII's reign, as will be noted, were providence and compassion. An inscription says of him: "He suffered from the sicknesses of his subjects more than from his own: for it is the public grief which makes the grief of kings and not their personal grief." The Khmers, and their kings especially, were concerned about sickness and its treatment. Doctors had existed since pre-Angkor days: the death of a doctor in 639 inspired a panegyric inscribed on a stone found at Sambor on the Mekong River, and an inscription from the time of Yasovarman I says that the hermitages established then had a duty to provide medicine and food for the sick. Jayavarman VII ran what might almost be called a health service.

The inscription of Ta Prohm reveals that there were 102 hospitals in the Khmer empire when Jayavarman VII reigned. A number of hospital sites have been identified, by inscriptions or by the resemblance of certain ruins to sites where these inscriptions have been found. The architectural features of Khmer hospitals are well known. The actual sickrooms, made of wood, have perished, and all that remains now is the religious center of each hospital. A tower opened to the east with a forecourt, and southeast of this tower an annex chapel opened to the west with a forecourt. A wall protected these buildings, and there was usually a pool outside the wall. One of these hospital sites has been located at Say Fong near Vientiane, and is the farthest known point of Khmer expansion north of Angkor. It lies downstream from Vientiane, just around the second bend, and on the north bank, of the Mekong

River, shortly past the island of Dong Noy. The Laotians referred to the region until lately as "Khmer bridge." A hospital site in northeast Thailand yielded part of a bronze mirror frame, the personal gift of Jayavarman VII to "the holy hospital of the district of Virendrapura."

Remains of the chapels serving four hospitals have been found outside the walls of Angkor Thom at the four cardinal points of the compass. Outside the east and west gates of the city these ruins are now known simply as hospital chapels. The chapel outside the north gate is called Prasat Tonle Snguot, and the one outside the south gate (in fact, it lies close to the northwest corner of Angkor Wat's enclosure) is known as Ta Prohm Kel. The medical personnel in each hospital consisted of two doctors, two pharmacists, fourteen guardians, eight male nurses, and six female nurses, all of whom were lodged in the hospital itself. In addition, there were six orderlies (one male and two female orderlies for each doctor), two cooks, two pounders of rice, two clerks, and sixty general assistants, all of whom were lodged outside the hospital and worked in shifts. Two priests and an astrologer completed the staff of more than a hundred. Inhabitants of the country immediately surrounding a hospital were specially privileged. "Even if guilty of repeated crimes," ordered Jayavarman VII, "the inhabitants of this place must not be punished; but those persons must be punished without mercy who take pleasure in harming living beings."

The Cambodians practice an enormous number of old wives' remedies, some of which must come from their Khmer heritage. Most of these remedies involve the use of leaves or tree bark. Some are more fantastic. Python's bile mixed with water is a cure for ulcers. Cat's excrement is made into a potion for asthmatic persons. Rusty iron filings are prescribed for venereal diseases. A mixture of elephant, white horse, and albino-buffalo bile is supposed to stop hiccups. A cure for dengue and other fevers contains fifteen ingredients, including powder made from deer's horn, ivory, and tiger's tooth.

The Khmers had the same kind of remedies, if not the actual ones known to the Cambodians. An inscription lists thirty-one different medicines, many of which seem to be types of food intended to give the patient nourishment and to help him build up his strength naturally rather than to cure him medicinally. A stone used for scraping and preparing medicines has been found in Takeo province. The actual treatment of sick persons is shown on the Bayon bas-reliefs. An ill subject lying on his left side clutches an enormous cushion, perhaps to relieve the tension of pain. His right leg is twisted in agony over the left leg. Two persons assist at this sickbed. One runs his fingers soothingly over the patient's forehead, and the other calls for help. When illness resulted in death, the Khmers were filled with grief—even though death might be the prelude for a more satisfactory rebirth. The frieze of Angkor Wat shows monkeys filled with quasi-human grief as they stand around the deathbed of their king.

Fig. 31 Angkor Wat: an episode from the *Ramayana* depicting the death of Hanuman, the monkey king (*Mavis Cameron*).

Lepers were a common sight at Angkor, but according to Chou Ta-Kouan they were not outcasts. He says, too, that one of the earlier Khmer kings had been a leper. Jayavarman VII's interest in hospitals, his sympathy for the sick, and the emphasis in sculpture at this time on providential deities have made some students think that he was himself a leper. There is no evidence for this, however. The statue of the Leper King, discovered at Angkor Thom, does not portray Jayavarman VII. His interest in the sick simply reflected a general concern for health problems. His deformed foot may have served as a constant reminder.

This, then, was the manner in which the ancient Khmers played out their lives. The day-to-day pattern has been reconstructed with caution and against obstacles. We know that all statements are useless unless a feeling for the evidence is preserved. Throughout this account, therefore, we have cited archaeological, historical, sociological, and geographical evidence wherever possible—objects discovered, inscriptions (see Plate 36), accounts of Chinese travelers (especially those of Chou Ta-Kouan), temples and statues, Cambodian customs, climatological studies of Indochina—all elements that might be germane. Many details are still lacking, of course. One can only hope that future discoveries may continue to fill in missing bits of the puzzle and heighten our understanding of this singular people.

## Chapter 6

### Angkor Wat

During most of the first half of the twelfth century, the Khmers were ruled by Suryavarman II. Supported by an astute priest, he engaged in the construction of a temple so strangely beautiful that its very name today conjures up the word genius. Neither he nor the future ruler Jayavarman VII—then a boy—could have foreseen that this edifice, now known as Angkor Wat, would far outweigh all the other glories of their dynasty.

The influential priest was named Divakarapandita. The suffix *pandita,* from which the word "pundit" is derived, signified "learned priest." Born in a small provincial village in 1040, Divakarapandita became a member of one of the teaching corporations established by Udayadityavarman II and achieved official standing while he was still a young man. He served Harshavarman III, but later taught Jayavarman VI. This move itself prefigures the tactics of an opportunist, since the latter ruler had usurped the throne of the former. As Divakarapandita advanced in power, he was rewarded with a gold palanquin and a white parasol, and charged with distribution of various gifts to the temples on behalf of the king. An inscription tells us that he accompanied his master on many journeys and made sacrifices.

When Jayavarman VI died, the high priest consecrated Dharanindravarman I, a reluctant monarch, who, after only five years reign, was overthrown by his nephew in 1113. The priest, now having served two factions, must have been indispensable to the next usurper—Suryavarman II. His rewards included a more fanciful palanquin and two peacock-feather fans with gold handles. Such fans are frequently depicted on the bas-reliefs of Angkor Wat, which was planned as the devaraja temple-mountain of the king. Divakarapandita continued his functions for many years, distributing gifts in various temples, presiding over rituals and digging a reservoir at Wat Phu, which was named after him (see Fig 3, p. 35). To honor his eightieth birthday, special decorations were ordered for his native village. It was with the backing of this powerful priest that Suryavarman II embarked on the building of the largest temple the Khmers had ever seen.

To explorers, archaeologists, and writers, Angkor Wat has always been the epitome of Khmer civilization. To Henri Mouhot, rediscoverer of Angkor, it was built by some ancient Michelangelo. To Louis Delaporte, explorer of Khmer ruins, its builders were the Athenians of the Far

East. Like all great masterpieces, it has inspired farfetched speculation and crankishness. An American lady visitor decided to leave her money to the archaeologists if they would receive her ashes for scattering among the ruins. One writer injected himself with mescaline to insure that his book on Angkor might be a peak performance. Then he wrote in all banality that Angkor Wat was "one of the most lovely pieces of architecture in the world." The superlative nature of the structure seems to defeat every attempt to describe it. Loti on Angkor is dim; Sitwell on Angkor is bizarre. Even Mouhot longed for the pen of a Chateaubriand or the brush of a Claude Lorrain.

The rough-and-ready translation of the words Angkor Wat as "the temple which is a city" has caused confusion. Besides remembering that Angkor Thom is a city and Angkor Wat a temple—both on different sites—we should also bear in mind that these places were not referred to as Angkor in ancient times—at least not as a place name. Angkor, derived from nagara, the Sanskrit word for "city," has become a place name by usage, just as part of London is known as the City. Ancient cities in the Angkor region are clearly labeled, including two on the Angkor Thom site whose ancient names are unknown but which were centered respectively on the Baphuon and on the later Bayon. Cambodians sometimes refer to Angkor Thom as "Big Angkor" and to Angkor Wat as "Little Angkor." (In Cambodian, Angkor Thom really means "Big Angkor," whereas Angkor Wat means "Angkor Monastery.")

Madeleine Giteau has written that the genius of Angkor Wat is of a type one does not dissect. It is reasonable, however, to dissect it and to ask in particular whether it looks now much as it did in ancient times. The gray bud-shaped towers, the dark and dank corridors, the shiny black bas-reliefs, the moat covered with water hyacinth, the bare rooftops, and the presence of saffron-robed Cambodian monks lull us into believing that this is the Angkor Wat which any Khmer would have recognized.

Actually, the saffron-robed monks of Theravada Buddhism were not established at Angkor until after the reign of Suryavarman II. And the sculptured lions which stand on the western causeway of Angkor Wat, as well as at other salient points inside the temple, were originally painted in brilliant colors, chiefly gold and red. Even in their present state, the lions of Angkor Wat are grander than any others in Khmer sculpture because of their erect stance and their slightly elongated backs. They contrast with the earlier lion statues found at Preah Ko, Phnom Bakheng, and Banteay Srei, which crouch lower on the ground and are clumsier in appearance. The lion is not native to Indochina, and the heads of lions in Khmer art are not realistic. Yet the Khmers regarded the lion as a *dvarapala* (guardian) and as the animal which carried the throne on which Vishnu or Indra sat.

The moat which stretches from either side of the western causeway and surrounds Angkor Wat once formed part of the main irrigation system of Angkor. On its east side it was linked by canals to the Siemreap River, and on its north side it was linked to canals which were themselves part of the irrigation works south of Angkor Thom. The fast-growing weed water hyacinth, which threatens to cover the surface of Angkor Wat's moat, did not exist there in ancient times (see Plate 4). It has only recently begun to flourish in Indochina's waters, and its stalk, when compounded with small crabs, is used by Cambodians as a cure for diarrhea. Lotus, not water hyacinth, grew on the waters in the time of Suryavarman II.

There are four entrance gateways to Angkor Wat, two of which—the east and west—are approached by causeways over the water (see Plate 1). They are called *gopuras,* a term also used for the pyramidal towers over entrances of temples in south India. At Angkor Wat they were just entrances—of simple cruciform design in the east, south, and north, but elaborated into five crosses with bays and false doorways in the western, main entrance. The roofed arcades, which form a rectangle linking the gopuras, were once adorned with stone finials similar to those that have been restored at Banteay Samré (see Plate 3). They give a spiky appearance to the rooftops (see Plate 20).

Henri Parmentier, one of the many architects who have worked on Khmer ruins, drew attention to the proportional reduction which the Khmers used when designing

their temples. The heights of the recesses in their pyramidal temple-mountains and the lengths between the edge of
one recess and the base of the next were reduced propor-
tionally toward the center. This means that the central
tower of Angkor Wat, when viewed from the western
causeway, does not seem to rear up from a backward or
forward position. It rises fairly and squarely from the center of its pyramid, and is not obscured by either of the two
recesses below it. Angkor Wat, when dissected, is composed of major towers set on an artificial recessed pyramid
and of minor towers crowning continuous galleries. In this
context, major towers are defined as those which surround
the central shrine or are themselves central shrines, and
minor towers as those which are set apart from the central
sanctuary.

Major towers had always been a feature of the Khmer
temple-mountains—for example, the five towers of Ta
Keo or the single tower of the Baphuon. The artificial recessed pyramid, such as the Bakong or Prasat Thom of
Koh Ker, had for a long time been a regular feature, too.
As for galleries, Pré Rup (A.D. 961) had noncontinuous
galleries (i.e., halls), and earlier temples, Phnom Bakheng
(ninth to tenth century) and the Bakong (A.D. 881), had
no galleries at all. Both the Bakong and Phnom Bakheng
had minor towers, as did later temples (Pré Rup and the
East Mebon). All these elements were blended harmoni-
ously in Angkor Wat, especially the galleries, which besides being continuous fit into the general scheme. The
towers, too, contributed to the pattern. In Ta Keo, the five
towers stood free, but in Angkor Wat they were linked by
a continuous series of porches and small chambers, with
steps leading to the center. This architectural formation,
besides providing the third and final recess of the artificial
pyramid, also repeated on a smaller scale the continuous
galleries of lower recesses. There were no loose ends, and
each part was integrated with the whole.

The Khmers were fettered by tradition. Although the
physical expression of their ideas reached perfection in
Angkor Wat, the idea behind Angkor Wat was the same as
that which had animated Phnom Bakheng or the still earlier temples of pre-Angkor days. Just as the idea was the

same, so the Khmers believed that the places themselves
were the same. Thought was the alternative to sight. The
Khmers' thinking was only as flexible as a man's gaze
raised high enough to glimpse Mount Meru or lowered
until it rested on the waters below. Successive temple-
mountains in different locations were different aspects of
the same thing. Angkor Wat was Phnom Bakheng, which
was Sambor Prei Kuk. The builder of Phnom Bakheng
merged with the builder of Angkor Wat. Both temples
were dwellings of the same divine personage, and, in essence, there could be no great difference between the Siva
of Phnom Bakheng and the Vishnu of Angkor Wat.

The five towers of Angkor Wat are arranged like the
five points on a die (see Plate 6). The steps leading to the
central tower are much steeper than the steps of an earlier
temple like Preah Ko. The central tower, loftier than the
other four, is higher than the central tower of the later
Bayon but probably lower than the height of Ta Keo.
Originally, these towers were painted gold and white. An
inscription refers to the splendid colors of the towers of a
temple after refreshing contact with the clouds. In other
words, gilt towers gleamed after rain. There may also have
been upturned tridents on the towers—attributes of Siva.
Bells used by the priests when performing rites were sometimes decorated with a trident that served as a handle.
Though Chou Ta-Kouan does not mention that there were
tridents on the towers of Angkor Wat, a bas-relief of the
Bayon shows three towers surmounted by them.

The history of an ancient civilization is often illuminated by a study of its art styles. This is partly true of the
Khmers, and the Angkor Wat style of statuary, though not
outstanding, has a place. Art historians have given names
to its progressions. In Jayavarman II's day the Phnom
Kulen style prevailed. Statues had cylindrical diadems that
looked like columns. Later, these gave way to recessed
diadems which recall the recesses of the temple-mountains
themselves. In the reign of Indravarman I—style of Preah
Ko—the legs of male statues do not have realistic muscles.
This became more pronounced in the Phnom Bakheng
style—reign of Yasovarman I—in which drapery on
statues runs in a series of stiff, angular folds. The wooden,

loglike appearance extends to the waist, and even above the waist Bakheng statues are rigid. Facial features such as eyebrows, mustache, and beard are emphasized in stark lines. Recessed diadems begin to be elaborately decorated.

The Koh Ker style—reign of Jayavarman IV—is vigorous when compared with the stylized, primitive statues of earlier reigns. Garuda walks upright without any support. Similarly, a lion stands on its hind legs. A group of wrestlers are locked together in dynamic action (see Plate 57). There is less stylization, and the conical recessed diadem appears for the first time, looking like a sleeping volcano. The two styles which follow, Banteay Srei and Kleangs— reign of Jayavarman V—are marked by a certain prettiness bordering on mannerism and by a return to earlier styles—smooth drapery, dating from pre-Angkor statuary, and a loss of vigor (see Plate 51). Then comes the Baphuon style—reign of Udayadityavarman II—distinguished by a slenderness in the bodies of statues and an oval chubbiness in their faces. Hairstyles reproduce the appearance of recessed diadems and are held in chignons by circular rings.

This was the background from which the sculptors of Angkor Wat drew inspiration for the celestial dancers in the upper courtyard. Their infinitely varied hairstyles and headdresses give them a distinct charm, but from a stylistic point of view they do not mark any great advance. Faces are less chubby than those of the Baphuon style and resume a more angular appearance. Their legs and drapery are somewhat stylized, and their lack of realistic muscle recalls earlier modes. To the Khmer, these changes of style were not significant. The intensity with which an image was worshiped never changed. The central statue of Angkor Wat, a Vishnu which has perished, had an immutable meaning. A small bronze statue of Siva could be the same Siva as the gigantic linga of Koh Ker. The tortoise at the base of the churning legend sculptures was the same Vishnu who rose in human form on a higher register of the same frieze. Nor did the complicated development of artistic styles reflect any rise or fall of the Khmer empire. Art developed in its own wayward fashion. The chief index of Khmer prosperity was size and number. The bigger a temple, the greater the number of statues—these things reflected the importance of the builder-king and the wealth of his period. With Angkor Wat, Khmer architecture reached a new summit, but Khmer statuary looked backward. However, there was one area of Khmer art in which the builders of Angkor Wat excelled: the frieze.

A Cambodian manuscript of recent date describes the walls of Angkor Wat as being "without any empty space." This is a fair description of the four great galleries sculptured with bas-reliefs (see Plate 5). The dark, dank corridors, with their figures black as ivory, were once hung with brilliant draperies. The sculptured frieze itself was painted in contrasting colors. The throng of figures on this frieze led the German critic W.O. Grob to suggest that the Khmer sculptors felt a greater kinship with the masses than with their king. The crowding of figures does make these bas-reliefs obscure and difficult to follow in cartoon strip fashion. But this has nothing to do with kinship for the masses. The frieze would be much easier to follow if space had been left between figures, but spaces would have detracted from the sculptors' main objective—the construction of a wall. This wall, forming one of the recesses of the temple-mountain, had to be the important functional limb of an architectural body and yet not detract from the building as a whole.

Faced with the rubric that there should be no empty space on the frieze, the Khmers resorted to other methods of highlighting the main figures. In a scene from the *Mahabharata* that shows Bhisma, who has just been attacked by Arjuna, the figure of Bhisma is stretched out and surrounded by arrows. According to the legend, Bhisma is pierced by so many of Arjuna's arrows that when he falls from his chariot the arrows act as a kind of couch, holding him up from the ground. On the frieze, his body is surrounded by these arrows, laid out as some eighty parallel lines above and below. From the spectator's point of view these lines appear as shading, effectively highlighting the body of Bhisma. The result is similar to that which would have been obtained by leaving space. Elsewhere on the frieze important personages stand out less effectively from the welter of figures.

The themes depicted on the frieze are taken from the Hindu epics, especially from the legends concerning Vishnu. Gallery D illustrates the all-important churning legend, and Gallery E is thought to depict two armies marching on Vishnu. In Gallery F, there is an incident from the *Harivamca,* an epic poem dealing with the genealogy of Vishnu, in which Krishna conquers Bana, a confederate of Siva. Garuda is seen battling his way through the wall of flame surrounding Bana's stronghold. In Gallery F, Vishnu appears mounted on Garuda; he is dramatically framed by four prancing horses. The frieze in Gallery G is identified as the Siege of Lanka, from the *Ramayana.* It portrays a series of duels in which combatants strike at each other with rocks and trees. The central duel takes place between Rama, the avatar of Vishnu, and Ravana, Vishnu's enemy. The monkeys, who are fighting on Rama's side, are depicted with enormous vigor. Each main gallery is divided into two sections, identified here by letters running from A (south section facing west) in a counterclockwise direction round the building to H (north section facing west).

The word "Paramavishnuloka" is clearly legible on the bas-reliefs of Angkor Wat. Although it was known that "Paramavishnuloka" referred to a royal personage in Gallery B, it was not at first possible to pinpoint this as a posthumous name for Suryavarman II. However, an inscription from Pimai, one of the centers of Khmer kings at this time, mentions an official of Dharanindravarman I whose name also occurs on the walls of Angkor Wat and who has been identified as one of the dignitaries in the royal procession of Gallery B. This official survived the death of his first master and entered the service of a new master, the Paramavishnuloka of Angkor Wat, Suryavarman II.

For some reason, the Khmers associated the worship of Vishnu with the west. We have already noted the bronze statue of Vishnu that was the central image on the West Mebon, the island temple in the West Baray. At the Bayon, Vishnuite scenes are sculptured on the west face of the interior gallery. Angkor Wat faces west and has its main entrance on the west side. Phnom Bakheng and the Baphuon, dedicated to the lingas of Siva, opened to the east. F. D. K. Bosch argues that Angkor Wat opened to-

Fig. 32  Angkor Wat: Bana, Gallery F bas-relief (*Mavis Cameron*).

ward the west because its builders wanted an entrance which could easily be reached from the road. If the temple had its main entrance on the east side, the approaches to it would be barred by the Siemreap River. A road led south from the city, and access to this road, Bosch suggests, was important.[1] This theory is questionable, however, for at the time of Suryavarman II there was space on either side of the road. The builders of Angkor Wat consciously chose an area east of the road so that the entrance could be made to open west in honor of Vishnu.

[1] F. D. K. Bosch, "Le temple d'Angkor Wat," *Bulletin de l'École Française d'Extrême-Orient*, XXXII (Hanoi, Vietnam, 1932), 19, n.4.

In order to investigate the possible purposes of Angkor Wat, archaeologists excavated the central tower. Study of the central tower of any Khmer temple is an obvious course of action, but with Angkor Wat there was a special reason. The most striking example of all such towers on Khmer temples, it was also the best preserved. Excavating it promised the diggers a chance to explore the foundations of a Khmer temple-mountain below the level where treasure hunters pursued their quests for loot.

Angkor Wat is famous for its bats, and when the tower was opened in 1909, a quantity of bat guano had to be removed. Some fragments of statues were discovered, including pieces of a large pedestal on which an important statue of Vishnu had once stood. At the second excavation, in 1934, more debris was removed, a treasure hunters' pit discovered, and various objects unearthed. One of these was a kind of sarcophagus. Coedès has acceptably defined Angkor Wat as follows: "Angkor Wat is the last dwelling of a being who enjoyed during his lifetime certain divine prerogatives, and whose final assimilation as a god was completed by death." [2] In other words, besides being a temple-mountain and the center of important irrigation works, Angkor Wat was also the funerary temple of Suryavarman II.[3]

In a sense, the most exciting part of the excavation had not yet begun. There might well have been further discoveries below the treasure hunters' pit, and so later in 1934 excavation was resumed. The diggers reached a depth of more than fifty-three feet from the top during this third attempt. In February, 1935, a new effort was made, which brought the level of excavation down to seventy-five feet.

[2] George Coedès, "La destination funéraire des grands monuments Khmèrs," *Bulletin de l'École Française d'Extrême-Orient,* XL (Hanoi, Vietnam, 1940), 342.

[3] Controversy once raged over whether Angkor Wat was the temple or the tomb of Suryavarman II. Jean Przyluski, in the *Journal of the Indian Society of Oriental Art,* V (Calcutta, 1937), 134, wrote: "Before one decides between the words 'temple' and 'tomb' the question must be asked whether the rites which took place there were offered to the remains of a mortal or the relics of a god." Coedès replied (*vide supra,* p. 340) that this was not a logical distinction, and that it was possible for the building to be regarded as both a temple and a tomb. The rites performed there are unknown.

Trouvé, who was in charge of the excavations, discovered two pieces of undressed laterite, in the lower of which was a circular cavity. Two pieces of crystal and two gold leaves lay in the cavity. There were also signs of four more square gold leaves, one of which still remained. This treasure was the original sacred deposit placed under the central tower of Angkor Wat when the temple was built. Every temple-mountain had its sacred deposit buried deep in the center. This was one of the prescriptions laid down in the manuscripts. Unfortunately, the manuscripts themselves, if any were placed under the central tower of Angkor Wat, have perished.

There is one feature of Angkor Wat which we have not yet mentioned—the *naga* balustrades. Although the churning legend is not depicted in them as in the figures with serpents outside the gates of Angkor Thom, these serpent balustrades, which run toward the temple along its western causeway and which break off periodically with their great fans of heads, are suggestive. Angkor Wat was more than the extension of an irrigation system, but like earlier Khmer temples, it still presided over the rice fields. There are some tiny carved motifs on the walls of Angkor Wat which seem at first purely decorative circular scroll patterns. Closer inspection reveals figures, either human or animal, in the center of each carving. One of these carvings depicts the churning legend in miniature, and another reveals the same legend *without* its serpent. We are reminded of the popularity of this legend by the bas-reliefs of Gallery D. The snake, whether by itself or in connection with the churning operation, was the all-important lord of the waters. Suryavarman II, the god-king of Angkor Wat, provided the water which would irrigate the rice fields and the magic which would insure a good crop.

As the size of Angkor Wat reflected the prosperity of the kingdom under Suryavarman II, the number of other temples built in a comparable style also attested to the Khmers' well-being. Banteay Samré, Thommanon, and Chau Say Tevoda were built at Angkor, while Beng Mealea and Preah Khan of Kompong Svay were begun in the provinces. All these temples repeat to some extent the architectural ideas of Angkor Wat. Banteay Samré has a central tower surrounded by four gopuras linked by galleries, and a long room between the tower and the east gopura. The central sanctuary of Thommanon consists of a single tower between the east and west gopuras and a long room linking the tower to the east gopura. Chau Say Tevoda is similarly planned, but with four gopuras. Although these temples are minute compared with Angkor Wat, they display the same integration of elements. By contrast, Beng Mealea and Preah Khan of Kompong Svay are huge enclosures. The inner perimeter of Beng Mealea is only an eighth shorter than that of Angkor Wat. Preah Khan of Kompong Svay covers the largest area of any Khmer building. Eight and a half square miles in area, it is even larger than the city of Angkor Thom itself. Much of the area within Preah Khan of Kompong Svay was given over to rice production. The integration of galleries and towers in Beng Mealea and Preah Khan of Kompong Svay recalls Angkor Wat, but since both provincial temples are laid out on a flat plan and do not rise up into a recessed pyramid, they are less impressive (see Plate 27). The encroaching forest has made their great size imperceptible to the passing traveler (see Plate 28). Although these monuments cannot be taken in at a glance like Angkor Wat, they too reflect the power of Suryavarman II.

In 1128 the Khmers marched through a mountain pass in the northeast and challenged the Annamite garrison at Nghean. Similar expeditions were made four years later in 1132, again in 1137, and again in 1150. The campaigns were not wholly successful, but they indicate that Khmer influence was felt by the Annamites in the far northeast. Ma Touan-Lin, the Chinese chronicler, reports several Khmer embassies to the Chinese court: one in 1116, made up of two envoys with a suite of fourteen retainers, which stayed till 1117, and another in 1120.[4] Suryavarman II also tried to put his own nominee on the throne of Champa. This activity in foreign affairs was a sign of the times. The Khmers were anxious about their frontiers.

When Suryavarman II died, about 1150, a Buddhist king, Dharanindravarman II, succeeded him. He was overthrown by a usurper, Yasovarman II, who was himself over-

4 Ma Touan-Lin, *Ethnographie des peuples étrangers*, p. 487.

thrown. An inscription says specifically that Yasovarman II was robbed of his throne by an ambitious servant, and it appears that by about 1165 Tribhuvanadityavarman was ruling at Angkor. These usurpations of power sapped the Khmers' morale and plunged them into dangerous domestic quarrels. From another inscription, about an independent king in Louvo (Lopburi), we understand that the outlying provinces of the Khmer empire were slipping away. A hostile king came to the throne of Champa and launched several invasions of Khmer territory, which led to the sack of Angkor in 1177.

The bas-reliefs of Angkor Wat and the Bayon provide a wealth of information about how the wars were waged (see Plate 16). The soldiers wore helmets, sometimes decorated with an animal's head. Their weapons were lances, sabers, axes, cutlasses, and bows. On land, catapults went into action from the backs of elephants or trailers. In river battles, the longboats were equipped with grappling irons and boarding parties. Heavy wooden truncheons also proved to be useful weapons. To defend themselves, the Khmers and Chams had shields and bucklers which strapped over the shoulder or wrist. They were made of plaited cane or wood, with carved wood and metal fittings. Elephants carried the warriors into battle by land. The longboats, whose prows were carved with Garuda and with other traditional motifs, were propelled by a double row of oarsmen. A bulwark of plaited cane protected them from the attacks of the enemy. The bas-reliefs of battle scenes are an outstanding example of how much has been learned of the details of Khmer life from the great temples.

# Chapter 7

## Height and Decline

The reign of Jayavarman VII marked the climax of Khmer history. During his time the greatest number of temples were built; irrigation systems were improved and extended to produce more rice than ever before; and the bounds of empire reached their greatest dimension. When Khmer troops finally vanquished their enemy neighbors the Chams, they were confirming the main theme of their king: victory. *Jaya,* the prefix of his name, meant "victory," and it was significantly coupled with other words: Jayatataka (Reservoir of Victory), Jayasindhu (Ocean of Victory), and Jayagiri (Mountain of Victory).

What sort of man was this Jayavarman VII? The stylized nature of Khmer sculpture would normally make even a superficial answer to such questions difficult, if not impossible. But a tendency of late twelfth-century sculptors to carve statues in the likeness of living people reveals this monarch in a way unusual in Khmer art. There are four representations of Jayavarman VII. The first is a statue found in a building to the southeast of the central sanctuary of Pimai; the second, found in two parts, shows body and head (see Plate 53). The third and fourth are heads only. The full statues depict a corpulent king with a deformed foot. He sits with legs folded in the attitude of Buddha. His eyes are closed and his lips fixed in an enigmatic smile. His drapery and hair style are extremely sim-

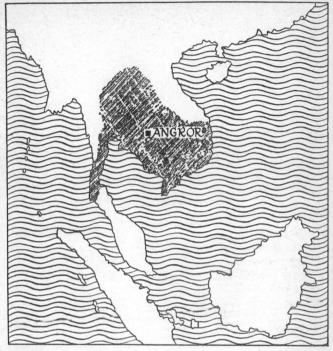

Fig. 33 The Khmer empire at its greatest extent *(John Stafford)*.

ple. The traits that emerge most powerfully are strength of
character and compassion.

On the military side, one of Jayavarman VII's first duties was to avenge the overwhelming defeat by the Chams
in 1177. He knew about the political situation in Champa
at first hand because he had led a force there much earlier
in the century and had even taken refuge in Champa when
affairs went badly for his family at Angkor. The Chams
had taken Angkor with their fleet, so the Khmers needed a
victory over them on the water. When a member of the
Cham royal family headed a rebellion in Malyang (general area of Battambang), the enemy seemed uncomforta-
bly close. Jayavarman subdued the region, then waged war
on Champa itself. In 1190 a Khmer prince defeated the

Chams at the king's behest, and their ruler was brought captive to Angkor. Jayavarman placed two rulers in command of the enemy kingdom, and the following year more fighting took place. A Cham king regained control of both capitals. This led to further attempts by the Khmer monarch to impose his rule, and by 1203 he was completely successful. For the next seventeen years, Champa was virtually a Khmer province, but the campaign had been a grueling affair. Nearly three decades had elapsed before the Khmers managed to wipe out the shame of 1177.

Fig. 34 Khmer helmet for an elephant going into battle (*Mavis Cameron*).

The sequence of Jayavarman VII's building program was as follows: public works, temples for ancestors, and a temple-mountain for the king. His chief public works were the construction of Angkor Thom and a redesigned irrigation system in the capital. The Khmers had been taken by surprise in 1177 because their city had no adequate walls. Jayavarman solved the problem of vulnerability by building a fortified square of laterite. These walls can still be traced through the forest. Sandwiched between the moat and a rampart of earth, they provided an imposing defense. As we mentioned previously, drains were built underneath them so that water could be fed into, and withdrawn from, the city system. Since the rampart lay within the city, sentries could patrol the walls by pacing the rampart. Small temples, the Prasats Chrung, were constructed at the four corners of the city's walls. The inscriptions of the king which they house refer to the wall fortress as his Mountain of Victory and to the moat as his Ocean of Victory. Some of these inscriptions are unfinished, which means that the king probably died before the northwest and northeast sections of the city were completed.

Jayavarman VII's ancestor temples were Ta Prohm and Preah Khan (Angkor). According to an inscription dating Ta Prohm as 1186, Jayavarman set up a statue there in honor of his mother. This sculpture was in the form of Prajnaparamita, the mother of all Buddhas. The central shrine of Ta Prohm consists of a tower linked by a long room to a series of towers, galleries, and chambers. These elements resemble Angkor Wat in general arrangement, but the temple does not rise on a recessed pyramid.

The second ancestor temple, Preah Khan, was not dedicated until 1191, and the inscription says that Jayavarman set up a statue there in honor of his father, Dharanindravarman II. This was in the form of Lokesvara. Like his father, Jayavarman VII was a Buddhist, and Lokesvara was the chief Buddhist deity portrayed during that period of Khmer sculpture. For the common people at Angkor, Lokesvara was the deity to whom they prayed for deliverance and who they hoped would intercede on their behalf. The many portrayals of the deity in this region were intended to reassure them that their empire was in the hands of a providential and compassionate spirit. Representations of the mother of all Buddhas, as well as a statue of Lokesvara, have been discovered in the ruins of Preah Khan. Today, both temples are like cemeteries. Sunk in the forest, they suggest an atmosphere of doom, decay, and death.

Other structures that Jayavarman VII erected were related to the expansion of irrigation works. Not only did the East and West Barays need to be revamped after the Champa invasion, but the water supply had to be increased through the addition of the North Baray and the Baray of Banteay Kdei. The North Baray, which the king called his Reservoir of Victory, lay to the east of Preah

Khan, and its water had to be hallowed in a unique way. The East and West Barays already had their island temples, known as the East and West Mebon.

The island temple of the North Baray is unique in Khmer architecture. It is called Neak Pean (Coiled Serpents) by the Cambodians because of the *naga* sculptures encircling its central sanctuary. When Angkor was rediscovered by explorers in the nineteenth century, a tree enveloped this tower and remained there until it was destroyed by a thunderstorm in 1935. Reliefs of Lokesvara found at the site provided the key to the island temple's purpose. Neak Pean was a center for ritual bathing, one method of obtaining the divine providence of Lokesvara for the Khmers. The central tower rises from the middle of a large pool, and four smaller pools surround it (see Plate 23). Each bank of the central pool forms the bank of a smaller one, and at the midpoint of each pool is a small chapel. Each chapel contains a carved stone gargoyle through which water could flow from the central pool into the four smaller ones (see Plate 24). Water entered the system by infiltration through the sandy bottom of the central pool, washing over lingas as it entered. This complex temple was inspired by a lake in Hindu mythology, located in the Himalayas, which gave birth to four great rivers through its gargoyles.

One of Neak Pean's statues, the horse Balaha, was found in fragments and has been reassembled in the central pool. It is the strangest Khmer statue in existence and a hallmark of Jayavarman's reign. In Buddhist mythology, the horse Balaha helps rescue five hundred merchants from drowning by inviting them to climb on his back and hang onto his mane. The Khmer statue depicts the merchants clambering for a hold on the horse (see Plate 25). They look upward in a helpless, expressive way which is rare in Khmer statuary, and one student of Khmer civilization has compared them to the Romanesque sculptures of St. Trôphime at Arles.[1] The horse became a symbol of protection for the Khmers, and, today, wooden ladders or

[1] Victor Goloubew, "Le Cheval Balaha," *Bulletin de l'École Française d'Extrême-Orient*, XXVII (Hanoi, Vietnam, 1927), 227.

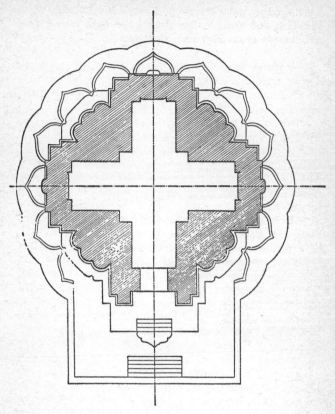

Fig. 35  Neak Pean: plan of the central tower showing lotus decoration *(after Marchal, EFEO)*.

stairways leading to the doors of Cambodian houses are often carved with a horse's head as a terminal motif. At Neak Pean, the horse Balaha expressed the idea of help and providence, so important to Jayavarman VII. Even today, the temple of Neak Pean appeals in a rare way to the emotions of Western visitors, and it has become one of their favorite haunts.

Like the greatest Khmer kings who preceded him, Jayavarman wished to build his own temple-mountain. He chose as a site the center of Angkor Thom, a point at which roads converged from the north, south, east, and west gates. The purpose of the temple-mountain was to give meaning to his subjects' labors. Here their hopes and aspirations were to be fostered, their fears and misgivings allayed. To do this, the king broke with a past tradition that the royal temple-mountain should be devoted to the devaraja. Instead of a linga or statues of Vishnu or Siva, he placed in this temple a statue of Buddha. The idea of devaraja persisted, but now the god-king had become a *buddharaja*, since the king was himself a Buddhist. Jaya-varman also wished to complete a trinity of temples which corresponded to a traditional Buddhist trinity: Lokesvara (Preah Khan), Prajnaparamita (Ta Prohm), and Buddha (the Bayon).

The central sanctuary of the Bayon, Jayavarman VII's temple-mountain, consisted of a recessed circular tower decorated with the faces of Lokesvara. A treasure hunter's well was discovered inside the central tower, and when it was excavated, fragments of a large seated Buddha were unearthed. A sacred deposit of gold leaf was found under-neath and, at the bottom, two fingers from a hand of the large statue. The *buddharaja* of Jayavarman VII still lay where it had been placed at the beginning of the thirteenth century.

Besides the central tower, there are numerous others bearing the faces of Lokesvara, all cramped for space. The stifling lack of space and the exaggerated emphasis on Lokesvara's face have earned the Bayon the doubtful honor of being called baroque. To Loti, the Bayon's towers seemed like giant pineapples placed end to end, and Paul Claudel, the French academician, saw them as some crazy kind of bowling pins (see Plate 11).

The statue of Buddha in the Bayon's central well and the repeated faces of Lokesvara on the towers were two means to Jayavarman's end. Since the king wished to im-press on all his subjects the importance of the *buddharaja*, appropriate statues were duly made in remote parts of the empire. The faces of Lokesvara were also reproduced, not only on the gateways of Angkor Thom but also on towers of distant provincial temples. Visitors to the Bayon from the provinces might miss the grand perspective of Angkor Wat, but they would note carefully the importance given to the Lokesvara faces. They recognized the resemblance between these face-towers and those in their own district. Indeed, the Bayon was like a collection of towers drawn from outlying parts of the empire. When the people paraded for their census in the open spaces at the center of Angkor Thom, they felt a sense of belonging because of these familiar towers. The Bayon might be a muddle artistically, but it had immense meaning for the common people. In its original state, it was painted a brilliant gold and was surmounted by a gold motif which has since been looted.

The bas-reliefs of the Bayon are different from those of Angkor Wat. The carving and composition are cruder, but the subject matter had greater appeal for the common people. There were fewer complex mythological scenes here and more representations from their daily life (see Plate 15). Ordinary folk, excluded from Angkor Wat by the priests, were allowed to circulate in the Bayon. They saw themselves depicted on the walls. They felt part of the royal plan. The smiles on the faces carved upon the towers may be described as mysterious and enigmatic. To visitors, they betokened good things to come. This was how the king associated the labors of his subjects with the central temple-mountain and gave meaning to their work.

For the Khmers, the Bayon was the ultimate expression of the churning legend; they hoped that the water would be churned and the longed-for gifts of prosperity conjured up. In simple terms, Jayavarman VII himself looked out over his people from the gateways of the city (see Plate 9), from the Bayon and from the many provincial temples. The water under the Bayon would be churned by the *buddharaja* into the valuable ambrosia. This was the epitome of the traditional way in which Khmer kings combined the needs of religion and the needs of the economy.

With a strong king at Angkor, the Khmer empire spread to its greatest extent. At first, Jayavarman consolidated the provinces. He developed the enormous centers begun in earlier times at Beng Mealea and Preah Khan (Kompong Svay). He also built Banteay Chhmar (see

Plate 30), which lies north of Sisophon, in the foothills of the Dangrek range. The Khmers had slaves from Burma, but the area covered by Burma today was never part of the Khmer empire. The Khmers always confined themselves to the Indochina peninsula. They were strongest in the area lying between the lower valleys of the Menam and the Mekong rivers. Their empire stopped short of the Malayan peninsula in the south and of the Red River delta in the northeast. In the central region they held sway as far north as Vientiane, and a Khmer statue has been found at Louang Prabang. They did not rule the mountains of Laos, nor did they penetrate into the mountains separating Burma and Thailand. The empire of Jayavarman VII was not the result of military expansion, though the Khmers defeated the Chams in the southeast and destroyed an Annamite fleet in the northeast. Their zone of influence was determined mainly by natural, not human, barriers: the sea (east and south), the mountains (north and northwest), and the isthmus of Kra (southwest). Although Jayavarman's armies were successful, the Khmer empire was comparatively small. When it fell, the Khmer army did not put up a stout resistance.

In order to run the Khmer empire smoothly, Jayavarman VII was aided by a hierarchy of public servants—corporation members who specialized in certain types of work and received privileges in return. Auditors, archivists, masters of public works, and many others made up a public service which the king himself controlled, enabling him to maintain a strong centralized administration at Angkor.

There were a host of minor functionaries such as guardians of the bedchamber, ushers, punka carriers, and so on. Although the period was marked by progress and order, Jayavarman's reign produced disorder, too. Most of his buildings were left unfinished. Some, like the temple of Ta Som, show haste and neglect in their decoration (see Plate 29). Roads were planned but not completed, many of the hospitals and rest houses were temporary, and Angkor Thom itself seems to have been left in a tentative state.

The Bayon shows discordant changes in the course of its construction, the final sprouting of towers reflecting chaotic haste. Its frieze is more crudely carved than that of Angkor Wat.

The Khmer empire under Jayavarman VII was like a plant grown under excessively artificial conditions or a creature forcibly fattened until it can hardly stand. The growth was too sudden and too spectacular to last. This ruler may be regarded as the greatest of Khmer kings, but his achievements were not as durable as those of some of his predecessors. An incident in the king's foreign policy illuminates his own uncertainty. The history of the Sung dynasty records that an embassy was sent to the Chinese court in 1200. The delegates were said to represent a dependency of Angkor, whose king had reigned twenty years. Obviously, the reference is to Jayavarman VII himself. The Chinese did not take his delegates seriously and regarded a memorial which they brought as a comic affair. Feeling that his empire had expanded too fast and might attract unwelcome attention from China, the Khmer king seems to have willfully deceived the Chinese; instead of sending his own delegation from Angkor, he sent laughable envoys from the provinces.[2] This story and the general lack of information about Jayavarman VII's reign in the thirteenth century, as opposed to the extensive documentation of his earlier period, are perplexing. A fairly late date, about 1218, is usually given for his death, but what he did between 1204 and 1218 is vague.

The unfinished buildings, the uncertainties which cloud Jayavarman VII's last years, are the background of a familiar question which is asked about the Khmers: Why did their civilization collapse? Angkor was dramatically abandoned, but the decline from the reign of Jayavarman VII onward was gradual. Chou Ta-Kouan did not arrive at Angkor until the end of the thirteenth century. He saw the splendor of the Khmers, but he saw, too, elements of

2 O. W. Wolters, "Chen-li-fu," *The Journal of the Siam Society*, XLVIII (Bangkok, 1960), 3; "Tambralinga," *Bulletin of the School of Oriental and African Studies*, Vol. XXI, No. 3 (London, 1958), 606.

decay. It was not his object to assess the Khmer kingdom as a power in Southeast Asia, but from his observations and from archaeological evidence we can see that the twelfth century, which began with the building of Angkor Wat and ended with Jayavarman VII's triumph over the Chams, was not really a golden age for the Khmers. Their resources had been stretched too far. Their religion, their economy, and the prestige of their god-king would—in the next century—be undermined.

## THE DOWNFALL OF THE KHMERS

Contrary to speculation, the Khmer empire did not decline because of internal decadence or a sybaritic way of life. Much opium is cultivated in the hills of north Indochina, but it is smoked by few Cambodians today, and this was also probably true at Angkor. Likewise, records of male prostitution[3] and later knowledge of homosexuality in Cambodia[4] do not indicate that deviation was prevalent at Angkor or a determining factor in its decline. The real reasons for the Khmer downfall lie in the empire's dismemberment from without and a loss of religious equilibrium within. Excessive temple building, with its tremendous demands on the Khmer people, may also be blamed.

After Champa detached herself and fell victim to Annamite attacks from the north, the chief menace to the Khmers was from newcomers to south Indochina. The Thais, a vigorous people, broke away from the southern border of China and gradually moved south, attracted by the fertile valley of the Menam River. They were already known to the Khmers, who administered the first Thai set-

---

3 Chou Ta-Kouan, p. 16.
4 J-P. Dannaud, *Cambodge*, Saigon, Vietnam, 1956, p. 45.

tlements in the Menam Valley. Bas-reliefs of Angkor Wat even show some Thai warriors marching in the Khmer army.

Throughout the twelfth century, and more particularly in the thirteenth, the Thais moved nearer and nearer to Angkor. Sometime after the death of Jayavarman VII, they overthrew the Khmer administration in the upper Menam Valley and established a strong capital at Sukotai. This had once been a vigorous Khmer settlement. Thai influence in Indochina grew rapidly under king Rama Khamheng, who ruled at Sukotai at the end of the thirteenth century and the beginning of the fourteenth. Although the civilizing influence of Angkor was felt by the Thais at this time, the Khmers lost political control of the area. A military clash was inevitable. A Thai-Khmer war broke out in the mid-thirteenth century, of which Chou Ta-Kouan writes: "They say that in the war with the Thais the whole population was forced to fight," and that "recently in the course of war with Thailand [the villages] were entirely devastated." [5] A more dangerous, peaceful invasion by the Thais was also taking place. "Recently," reports Chou Ta-Kouan, "the Thais came to settle in this country and devote themselves to raising silkworms or cultivating the mulberry tree." [6]

The Khmers tried to resist a long series of Thai invasions, but midway through the fourteenth century Angkor was attacked and occupied. When the Thais left, the Khmer kings reoccupied their palace site and built what is known as Palace IV. This was their last period on the Angkor palace site (1350–1430) before Angkor fell. The Thai invasions had a disastrous effect on the Khmer economy: able-bodied men were taken off as slaves, and the irrigation systems of Angkor ceased to work effectively. Excavations have shown that the Thais blocked canals at Angkor, so that the complex irrigation system was dislocated. As we explained earlier, when rice fields were not regularly flooded with mud-bearing water, erosion occurred, and, finally, laterite. As the irrigation systems ceased to function the production of rice dwindled. The

[5] Chou Ta-Kouan, pp. 34 and 32.
[6] *Ibid.*, p. 30.

number of men sent into slavery did not perceptibly re-
duce the mouths to be fed, and one annual harvest was
not sufficient to feed the Khmer population. In 1431 the
Thais sacked Angkor again; the following year the
Khmers abandoned the site.

As the empire of Jayavarman VII came under siege important changes in the religious framework were also taking place. The thirteenth century witnessed an outbreak of
iconoclasm at Angkor, a rare thing in Khmer history, and
a fact denied by Indian writers.[7] Many statues of the
Bayon were mutilated and other damage occurred (see
Plates 12 and 22). The iconoclasts must have been Brah-
manic sympathizers, because the images of Siva and
Vishnu seemed to escape injury. The compatibility of Mahayana Buddhism (Jayavarman VII's religion) with the
worship of Siva and Vishnu broke down, and there was
bitterness among priestly families at Angkor. Into this fertile seedbed of unrest came a new religion, one of the
chief elements in the Khmer downfall.

Theravada Buddhism came to Angkor in the mid-thirteenth century. Also known as Hinayana (Little Vehicle),
or Southern school Buddhism, it arrived by way of Ceylon
and Burma, where it had been studied earlier by monks.
First the Thais and later the Khmers accepted this new
religion. According to Chou Ta-Kouan, the monks who
adhered to Theravada Buddhism "shave the head, wear
yellow robes, leave the right shoulder uncovered, gird themselves in a skirt of yellow stuff and go barefoot." Shin Ta-
malinda, one of the Burmese monks involved in the graft-
ing of new ideas onto an old religion, was said to have
been the son of a Khmer king. The Khmers inherited the
new teachings with some enthusiasm. Members of the
farmer-builder-soldier class, especially, became Buddhist
monks, enjoying a status of life they could never have attained before. With yellow dye from a tree, they proceeded to color their rags saffron and preach ideas which
undermined the whole structure of Khmer society. The

---

[7] Manomohan Ghosh, in *A History of Cambodia*, p. 192, asserts
that Jayavarman VII was a syncretist who accepted all the religions
that were practiced. If, then, the Buddhists received no special fa-
vors from Jayavarman VII, there would have been no need for an
iconoclastic reaction against the Buddhist king after his death.

new converts maintained direct contact with Ceylon as well as with Burma, and Theravada spread from Angkor to Laos. Today, it remains the religion of four countries with common frontiers: Thailand, Burma, Laos, and Cambodia.

Sanskrit, chief religious language of Angkor, gradually died out. It was replaced by Pali, the language of Theravada Buddhism. An inscription containing twenty lines of Pali and thirty-nine lines of Khmer dates from 1309. But the Khmers, who were dependent on Burma and Ceylon for their Theravada ideas, did not make striking or original use of the Pali language. The intellectual atmosphere which had existed at Angkor for so long did not survive the arrival of the new religion. The reason was clear—Theravada Buddhism had cut the ground from under the Khmer kings and priests. The basis of their power had been denied.

Theravada came peacefully and insidiously. It was not thrust on the Khmers from outside but grew naturally from within. The exhaustion of the population made them ripe for conversion. Buddhism, Sivaism, and Vishnuism could no longer exist side by side. In particular, the idea of the devaraja, or even of a *buddharaja,* was inconsistent with Theravada thought. All the characteristics of the god-king—sole ruler, arbiter, commander in chief of the armed forces, the god whom everyone had to worship, divinely enthroned ruler, incarnate form of Siva, Vishnu, Brahma, or Buddha—were hateful to the worshipers of Theravada.

According to Theravada teaching, earthly empires were vain, disputes had to be settled by Buddhist law, the taking of life was forbidden—even in war, and Buddha was not a god to be worshiped. Princes and kings were expected to give up their riches and walk barefoot, begging their food as Buddha, a royal prince, had done in India. Since Buddha was a man and not a god, there could be no thought of consecrating a king with divine power. The faithful were urged to do good works in this life and hope for a better reincarnation in the next. Instead of praying to a bodhisattva, the Khmers were taught to feed the monks of Buddha. But even the monks were not considered divine.

These ideas ran counter to the prestige of the devaraja and the lavish way he planned the Khmer way of life. They undermined the position of the priests, who behaved with arrogance rather than humility. Although the Buddhist monks were later to gain a dominant position in Cambodian society, they never took over the role of Khmer priests, who helped the king in his endeavors and built up the resources of the empire.

Most devastating of all, the new religion struck at the heart of the Khmer economy. The Khmers did not distinguish between the magic of religion, helped by statues and temples, and the magic of nature, helped by sowing rice seedlings in fertilized rice fields. To them, there was one, undifferentiated, operation to follow. Just as a reservoir was necessary for irrigation, so it was essential that this reservoir be part of a religious foundation devoted to some god. The god-king organized the system, presided over it, and protected those who worked for him.

In the reign of Jayavarman VII, when the need to rebuild the empire after a Cham invasion seemed pressing, the syncretism of Mahayana Buddhism with the devaraja cult provided an extraordinary religious impetus for the superhuman effort needed in the reconstruction. Irrigation systems were repaired and expanded, while equally large-scale temples were built at Angkor and in the provinces. When the new religion undermined this springboard of action by appealing to an already exhausted people, the building program came to a halt. As the dikes and canals of Angkor fell into disrepair because of invasion, and possibly flood, the cultivation of rice was threatened. The Khmer empire collapsed, and Angkor, the great center of the Khmers since the ninth century, was abandoned.

There were other factors which may have contributed to the final debacle. It is often said that the Khmers exhausted themselves building temples, and the many unfinished ones of Jayavarman VII may confirm this. Surely, the vast amount of building in his reign must have placed an enormous strain on the farmer-builder-soldier class, which bore the brunt of the construction. The building of new temple-mountains ceased with Jayavarman's death, as if the people were still reeling from earlier building programs. Natural hazards are still another possibility for the final decline, and the most likely of these would have been serious floods. Wooden houses, at least, could easily be replaced after fires, and the Indochinese peninsula has never known volcanic eruptions.

When the five centuries of Khmer rule at Angkor are considered as a whole, it is clear that in the later periods the people found themselves fighting more wars with neighboring countries, especially with the Chams. Arnold Toynbee wrote of Angkor: "The Khmer civilisation, like so many other civilisations before and after it, wrecked itself by indulging in these mad crimes" (i.e., in imperialistic wars, scenes from which, Toynbee feels, dominate the bas-reliefs).[8] Yet the Khmers were not really a warlike people. Their move to Angkor was not the result of military aggrandizement. Unlike their forerunners, the people of Funan, the Khmers isolated themselves from the trading routes of Southeast Asia. To infer that they were never aggressors would be absurd, but they did not embark on useless warfare. Indochina, with its natural boundaries, provided an easily defensible kingdom for many years. Only when the Thais moved into this region did the Khmers find themselves fighting constant wars. The civilization of the Chams was a first cousin to that of the Khmers, and they also collapsed under pressure—Annamite pressure—from the north. Although the Khmers subdued Champa, their might was not founded on exploitation of the defeated Chams. The power of the Khmer people depended on the highly organized society of Angkor.

[8] Arnold Toynbee, *East to West,* London, 1958, p. 81.

## Chapter 8

◆

## Rediscovery of Angkor and the
## Khmer Heritage

Though Angkor was not abandoned until some two hundred years after the death of Jayavarman VII, the Khmers rapidly became a forgotten people before 1432. It is indicative that Marco Polo, who might have contributed a valuable account of their life in decline, did not even bother to visit Angkor. Indeed, at the height of the Khmer empire, merchants did not go up the Mekong River as a matter of course; when Angkor was abandoned, they had even less reason to do so.

The commonly held belief that the builders of Angkor disappeared in the fifteenth century, that the Khmers as a race ceased to exist, is patently untrue. Modern Cambodians are directly descended from these forebears, and their history from before the fall of Angkor until the nineteenth century is recorded in a body of manuscripts known as the Cambodian Annals or Chronicles. These are comprised of private records devoted to families and individual Buddhist monasteries, and official documents dealing with history and the royal family—including lists of kings. The names of Jayavarman VII's successors, known from late Khmer inscriptions, overlap but do not tally with the kings of the Cambodian Chronicles. These chronicles, written four or more centuries after the events they relate, contain much legendary material.

One of the legends describes how a particular succession took place at Angkor. The reigning Khmer king charged a certain cucumber gardener to reserve his entire crop of cucumbers for the royal table. The king also gave the gardener a weapon to use against thieves who might break into the garden and try to steal the cucumbers. Then the king, who seems by nature to have been suspicious as well as greedy, crept into the cucumber garden one night to make sure his orders were being obeyed. Following the king's instructions to the letter, the cucumber gardener apprehended the intruder and killed him. Then, as if to prove that the better man had won, the story goes on to say that the cucumber gardener became king forthwith. This legend, a favorite with Cambodians today, is also told in Thailand and Burma. In spirit, it is far removed from the severe world of Angkor's kings as we have seen it up to now. After Angkor was abandoned, squabbles and dynastic usurpations became more and more common; the power of the devaraja had been dissipated.

The Khmers moved from Angkor to Srei Santhor and then to Phnom Penh. They tried to rekindle their past glories by building on the tiny hill at Phnom Penh and by naming their king Suryavarman. After further defeats by the Thais, they moved the capital to Lovek, between Phnom Penh and the Great Lake. When Lovek had been sacked by the Thais, they moved a short distance to Oudong. Here the Cambodian kings, as we must now call them, established their court. Members of the Cambodian royal family are still buried at Oudong, and this is where their immediate forefather, Norodom, handed Cambodia to France in the second half of the nineteenth century. Finally, the Cambodian capital was moved back to Phnom Penh, where it remains today. The history of Cambodia from the fifteenth to the nineteenth century is gloomy. First the Thai armies, then the Thai and Annamite armies in turn, devastated the country and treated the Cambodian kings as puppets. The Khmer civilization fell into decay, but not before it had beneficially influenced the vigorous and growing culture of Thailand. Theravada Buddhism helped the descendants of Angkor's builders to accept their evil lot, but they knew that the time of their greatness had passed.

The story of Angkor itself now becomes mysterious and

incredible. It was, indeed, a lost city in the same sense that the ancient centers of the Americas were lost until explorers from Europe unveiled them. The extraordinary thing about Angkor was that the West did not really rediscover it until the middle of the nineteenth century, although, as we shall see, frequent references were made to a Cambodian lost city during the preceding three centuries. In the sixteenth century, Cambodia began to be known through the accounts and maps of European travelers, and from them some information about the lost city can be obtained.

Gaspar da Cruz, a Portuguese monk, was the first missionary known to have visited Cambodia.[1] He stayed at Lovek in 1556 and tried to convert the inhabitants. Spanish adventurers entered Cambodia in the second half of the sixteenth century. They all but repeated the exploits of Cortes in Mexico and of Pizarro in Peru. Their efforts ultimately failed, however, and by the seventeenth century the idea of taking Cambodia for Spain had been forgotten. Portugal or Spain could have colonized Cambodia with ease. A Latin Indochina was almost in the making. But because these attempts did not bear fruit, Portuguese and Spanish scholars never followed up the interesting first reports about Angkor which were brought back from Indochina in the sixteenth century. The best of these reports, which was passed on to Diogo do Couto, the chronicler of Portuguese India, is a meager document when compared with the wealth of material which eventually came out of Central America.[2]

Diogo do Couto, whose informant visited Angkor, devotes a chapter of his account to "the large, marvelous town which was discovered in the forests of the kingdom of Cambodia, its construction and its situation." He reports that in the middle of the sixteenth century the king of Cambodia was going on an elephant hunt and suddenly came upon some imposing deserted buildings in the forest.

[1] C. R. Boxer, ed., *South China in the Sixteenth Century,* London, 1953, p. 62 ff.

[2] Bernard-Philippe Groslier, *Angkor et le Cambodge au XVIe siècle d'après les sources Portugaises et Espagnoles,* Paris, 1958, pp. 68–74.

The description which follows makes it certain that these buildings were the ruins of Angkor Thom. The Cambodians' rediscovery of their lost capital at this time finds echoes in other writings of the sixteenth century. The Cambodian king decided that he would reoccupy Angkor and try to revive its past. Excavations on the Angkor Thom palace site have not shown traces of a sixteenth-century settlement, but certain evidence on the bas-reliefs confirms it. The frieze of Angkor Wat was never finished in the time of Suryavarman II. During the short reoccupation of Angkor in the sixteenth century, the Cambodian king used Thai masters of works to complete detail on the frieze (Galleries E & F). This was not a revival of the Khmer genius but a short-lived attempt to revive Angkor itself.

The tales of Cambodia's lost city evoked wondrous comment. Bartolome L. de Argensola, writing in 1609, says that "Angon" (Angkor) may be "the fantastic city of Plato's Atlantis" or that described in Plato's *Republic*. A scholar of Argensola's acquaintance was ready to ascribe the building of Angkor to the Roman emperor Trajan. Gabriel Quiroga de San Antonio, writing in the late sixteenth century, says: "There are plenty of Jews in the kingdom of China. These are they who built in Camboxa [Cambodia] the town of Angor [Angkor]." Marcello de Ribadeneyra, also writing at this time, repeated speculation that Angkor was built by Alexander the Great or by the Romans. Diogo do Couto was better informed than his contemporaries, but he also contributed a wild speculation: "It is certain that this kingdom [Cambodia] once belonged to the Chinese." The seeds of discussion about Angkor were by now sown in Europe, but they had not yet taken root.[3]

Spanish and Portuguese accounts of Angkor begin to die out in the seventeenth century, when the Dutch took their place as the chief explorers of Southeast Asia. But there are not many Dutch references to Angkor. A Dutch merchant, Gerrit van Wusthoff, made a journey from Cambodia to Laos in 1641. When he reached the area of Wat Phu, he noticed oxcarts which were going from Bas-

3 *Ibid.*, pp. 74–80.

sac to Honcker (Angkor). The letter of a Dutch envoy to
his superior officer in 1656 refers to "a beautiful and
pleasant locality Anckoor [Angkor] which the Castilians
and Portuguese call Rome." A Dutch map of Indochina at
this period indicates Phnom Penh but not Angkor. Once
again, reports of Angkor reached the Western world and
were ignored. The seventeenth century also witnessed a
Japanese mission to Angkor, probably before 1636, when
travel outside Japan was forbidden. One of the Japanese
envoys commissioned a map of Angkor Wat after he returned home. A surviving copy, executed in 1715, shows
the buildings in a wash of India ink and the moat in pale
indigo. As a plan, it is full of errors. In the seventeenth
century, English settlers also came to Cambodia. An unau-
thorized branch of the East India Company was established at Lovek from 1651 until 1656. The reports and
letters of its officials are mostly confined to commercial and
domestic matters.[4] The English retired from Cambodia without rediscovering Angkor or even being aware of its
existence.

In the second half of the seventeenth century, French
travelers, especially missionaries, began to arrive in Indochina. One of these writes in 1658 about a Cambodian
temple "which is supported on six thousand large stone
columns"—clearly not an eyewitness account. Some
twenty years later, another French missionary, Father
Chevreul, spent time in Cambodia and wrote as follows:
"There is a very old temple distant about eight days from
the station where I am posted, and I hope to make a small
journey there soon, if our Lord gives me the opportunity
and leisure to do so. This temple is called Onco [Angkor],
and is almost as famous among the gentiles of five or
six kingdoms as St. Peter's is in Rome among the
Christians. . . . Siam, Pegu, Laos, Tenasserim and some
other kingdoms come to make pilgrimages there notwith-
standing the fact that they may be at war."[5] This last
sentence is of crucial importance. It shows that to the in-

---

[4] For a summary of this subject see Christopher Pym, *Le Cambodge au XVIIe siècle d'après les sources Anglaises* (article in preparation).

[5] Groslier, p. 131.

habitants of Burma and the Indochina peninsula Angkor was not really lost at all. Angkor Thom had been invaded by the forest, but Angkor Wat continued an unbroken existence as a temple. Theravada Buddhists now regarded it, illogically, as their own shrine, and in the following centuries it continued to provide sanctuary for pilgrims of various sects.

At the beginning of the nineteenth century, Angkor was still unknown to the Western world, in spite of existing references to Angor, Honcker, Anckoor, and Onco. A most astonishing event took place when a French scholar, Abel Remusat, was attracted to the writings of Chou Ta-Kouan and translated them in 1819. Yet nobody connected Chou Ta-Kouan's account with the admittedly legendary Angkor. In other circumstances, explorers would have set off at once to Chen-La (Cambodia) and have made most dramatic discoveries. But Angkor still waited, undiscovered. A detailed map of Indochina prepared by a bishop in 1838 did not mark Angkor, but it did indicate an area described as Nocor Khmer Caomen (Ancient Kingdom of Cambodia), between latitudes 12–14 degrees north and longitudes 105–6 degrees east. French missionaries visited the ruins from time to time. The French missionary Pallegoix, in his description of Thailand, referred to the marvelous ruins of Nokorvat (Angkor Wat).[6] Charles-Émile Bouillevaux, another French missionary, visited Angkor in 1850 and wrote a short account of his travels. His *Voyage dans l'Indochine: 1848–56* was published in 1858, but it did not reach a wide reading public in Europe. The foremost rediscoverer of Angkor was the naturalist Henry Mouhot, whose diaries, published posthumously in various journals and finally in book form (1864), attracted worldwide attention.

It is ironic that Mouhot failed to obtain support in France for his proposed travels and had to go to London for assistance. His diaries carry this dedication written by his brother:

TO THE LEARNED SOCIETIES OF ENGLAND, WHO HAVE '

---

[6] *Ibid.*, p. 137.

FAVORED WITH THEIR ENCOURAGEMENT THE JOURNEY
OF M. HENRI MOUHOT TO THE REMOTE LANDS OF
SIAM, LAOS, AND CAMBODIA

His brother mentions that Mouhot was half English by
marriage and that "it was on the hospitable soil of England
that he met with that aid and support, which not only her
scientific men but the whole nation delight in affording to
explorations in unknown countries. . . ."

Like anybody arriving at the lost city of Angkor for the
first time, Mouhot was deeply moved and highly excited by
what he saw. He made a sketch of Angkor Wat which
shows that it had survived the onslaught of the encroaching
forest, though some bushes were growing on its terraces
(see Plate 7). He climbed Phnom Bakheng and looked toward the hills of Phnom Kulen. "All this region," he wrote,
"is now as lonely and deserted as formerly it must have
been full of life and cheerfulness; and the howling of wild
animals, and the cries of a few birds, alone disturb the
solitude." [7] The lost city of Angkor had been found. Mouhot continued his journey into Laos, where he died of fever
near Louang Prabang. It is a sobering experience to visit
his grave in the Laotian forest and to recall that solitude
which stayed with Mouhot until his death.

Though travelers of many nationalities followed quickly
in Mouhot's footsteps, the most important explorations
were made by the French. By 1909 more than two hundred
books and reports about Khmer civilization had been published—including sixty scholarly articles. But more than
three centuries had passed since the first European travelers
set eyes on Angkor: time and valuable evidence had been
lost. Fifty years ago the study of Angkor was still in its infancy. Some of the men who worked then—George Coedès
and Henri Marchal, for example—are still active today.[8]

---

[7] Christopher Pym, ed., *Henri Mouhot's Diary*, New York, 1967,
p. 97.

[8] Marchal was for many years curator of Angkor, and Coedès for
a long time directed the EFEO. I acknowledge a special debt of
gratitude to M. Coedès for kindly reading this book at an early
stage.

On March 9, 1900, a decree of the Governor-General of Indochina brought all types of ancient remains under the control of France. The French School of the Far East (EFEO) was formed, with Cambodia as one of its chief fields of activity. The ancient Khmer ruins were an astonishing spectacle. The most damage and destruction had been done by trees, especially the silk-cotton tree. Where wooden beams had collapsed or iron crampons had rusted away, earth was blown by high winds and seeds became implanted. Roots prized the blocks of sandstone apart, producing weird effects. It looked as though an octopus or giant spider were crushing the temples (see Plate 21). Man had built Angkor. Now it looked as if Nature was mocking man's achievement. The romantic embrace of trees and towers did not look haphazard, but it was. The green shoots grew steadfastly toward the light and away from the center of gravity. The roots did the opposite—growing away from the light and toward the center. This is why the roots of trees at Angkor grow into the buildings, then downward, deeper and deeper, while the trees themselves grow higher and higher, shutting out the light.

The sandstone of Angkor has weathered remarkably well, considering that some of the temples are more than a thousand years old. The blackness on the bas-reliefs of Angkor Wat is caused by the presence of dark brown lichens which make tiny chinks in the sandstone surface. In time, this crust turns black and wears down until it looks polished. The whitish and yellowish patinas seen on certain statues and on the temple of Ta Keo are caused by the discoloration of the micas and the cement, as well as by chemical modification of the feldspars. The dark patches on the stones of Banteay Srei are the result of oxidation of manganese from the rock itself. The red patina, more rarely seen, is caused by the sweating out of iron oxide from inside the stone. Other patinas, such as the green on the reliefs of Banteay Chhmar, are caused by the impregnations of encrusted clay. These discolorations disappear with cleaning.

Over the centuries, the agent most destructive to the sandstone has been water. The rain in tropical Cambodia not only contains more nitric acid than in temperate zones but also acquires carbonic acid, infused into the atmosphere by respiration from the tropical forest. As soon as the rainwater comes into contact with objects on the ground, other acids, especially those of vegetable growths, are intermingled with it. The most soluble element in sandstone is the carbonate of lime in its cement fraction. Water also causes the kaolinization of feldspars and the transformation of micas, rendering the whole stone more soluble in the course of time. Stagnant water rises up through the pillars of Angkor Wat and causes the sandstone to flake. This kind of erosion is conditioned by the amount of water in the atmosphere. If the air is excessively full of moisture, water is prevented from evaporating and creeps upward into the stone. The south galleries of Angkor Wat have suffered particularly because they are exposed to regular wind and rain.

Lichens, sap from trees, soil, heat, and the urine of bats also cause some degree of damage (see Plate 14). Moss digs its way into the sandstone and breaks it up. Tree sap corrodes the stone. Soil helps the forest obtain its hold, though paradoxically the trees themselves protect the sandstone from overheating in the tropical sun. When statues are daily exposed to the sun, external particles of the stone dilate, contract, and fall off. In Angkor Wat the urine of bats undergoes a chemical modification and gives off corrosive vapors.

The architects and archaeologists of France were faced with an immense task. Their main achievements have been the discovery, preservation, and study of ancient remains. Indochina is a notoriously difficult terrain in which to work, and the EFEO demands from its members an extraordinary degree of courage and perseverance. Dysentery, drowning, assassination by pirates, suicide, war service, strain from living in a tropical climate, and an airplane disaster have robbed the French School of men who had much to contribute in the field of Khmer studies. Nevertheless, a tradition of family service has helped the EFEO from one generation to the next. The names of

Fig. 36   Angkor Wat: erosion of carved pillars creeps up insidiously (*Mavis Cameron*).

Maspero and Groslier recur. Parmentier received help from his wife, Jeanne Leuba.

At Angkor, the EFEO faced an immense task of *dégagement* (the disentangling of Khmer monuments from vegetation and earth) and anastylosis (the reconstruction of temples, stone by stone, according to the particular needs and particular plan of each). Even from Angkor Wat, which was well preserved, wagon loads of earth and roots had to be removed. Anastylosis presented many problems, especially when stones from a particular temple might be scattered over a wide area. One of the keystones for Asram Maharosei was found at Phum Prei Phdau, a village nearly twelve and a half miles away. In the course of archaeological work, certain peculiarities of Khmer architecture were unveiled—for example, insufficient foundations for a gallery, and drains situated above the surface of the area which they were meant to drain. Although many ruined temples have had to be left as they were found, the work of *dégagement* and anastylosis has gradually progressed (see Plates 42 and 43). A network of modern roads enables visitors to circulate easily at Angkor, but a visit to provincial monuments is not so practicable.

Controversy is apt to become the spice of archaeology, and Angkor has had its fair share of the traditional suspicion with which students of one discipline view the students of another. Today, however, their mistakes and methodological rivalries are things of the past. The major unsolved controversy about the Khmers concerns the influence of India. Such questions as "Did the Khmers have castes?" and "Did the Khmers have original ideas on astronomy and the calendar?" remain to be answered.

The discovery of a lost city in Cambodia created more of a stir in France than did the actual unearthing of Khmer art (see Plate 55). Some of the first explorers were lukewarm about Khmer statuary, and much time was to pass before the canons of Khmer beauty were understood. Nevertheless one of France's earliest concerns was to bring objects from the lost city to Paris. "I could not contemplate these monuments," wrote the explorer Delaporte, "without feeling an ardent wish to make them known in Europe and to enrich our museums with a collection of Khmer antiquities" [9] (see Plate 56). When 120 huge packing cases were deposited in the courtyard of the Louvre, neither the authorities there nor anywhere else in Paris were able to house them. Eventually their contents were displayed at the Palais de Compiègne. In 1878, some Khmer pieces were exhibited alongside Egyptian and Chinese antiquities at the Trocadéro. The Musée Guimet, which today contains the finest collection of Khmer sculpture outside Cambodia, was founded at Lyons in the same year (later moved to Paris). Some good examples have also found their way into French museums in the provinces (see Plate 39).

The French colonizers could not bring Angkor Wat to France, but a model was made and exhibited in Paris for all to see. Wave upon wave of poets, artists, and writers who visited Cambodia were chastened by the appearance of Angkor Wat. Very few of them were able to express

[9] Louis Delaporte, *Vogage au Cambodge,* Paris, 1880, p. 12.

their feelings. As the work of unveiling Angkor proceeded, there were moments of high drama. Trouvé discovered the *buddharaja* statue. The central tower of Neak Pean was struck by lightning. Commaille was murdered. Sculpture disappeared mysteriously—smuggled out of Cambodia, so it was rumored. EFEO collections in Saigon were damaged by a typhoon, and later by sabotage. Angkor was bombed. Prisoners from Cambodian jails worked on the upkeep of their ancestors' temples—irony indeed.

The Cambodians nurse a tradition that Angkor is destined to be rebuilt by foreigners. The origin of this tradition is uncertain, but it used to be attributed to Marcello de Ribadeneyra, who wrote about Angkor in the late sixteenth century. B-P. Groslier has pointed out that the passage could be translated in several ways and did not necessarily refer to rebuilding.[10] Now that the Cambodians themselves talk about this tradition as though it really were true, we are not in a position to deny or confirm it. If there was such an ancient prophecy, then France has been fulfilling it. When Mouhot rediscovered Angkor, the Cambodians refused to believe that their own ancestors had been the builders. It had been built by Indra, they said, or by giants, or by the mythical Leper King. Some even felt that "it made itself." The Cambodians' lack of belief in their own great parentage was shared by others. How—it was asked—could a great nation like the Khmers have undergone such a metamorphosis? The question was ill-phrased.

In the literary sphere, Cambodia draws inspiration and nourishment from the rich past of Angkor. The Hindu epics, especially the *Ramayana,* still provide the subjects for recitations and theatrical performances. The Royal Cambodian Ballet performs episodes from the *Ramayana* before an invited audience in the palace at Phnom Penh. The costumes of these dancers, especially those designed for the woman in the troupe, are strikingly rich. When they dance, the performers' physiognomies recall the statues on the walls of Angkor Wat. Themes from the *Ramayana* are also reenacted by village theatrical troupes, with pleasing lack of self-consciousness in their performances. Fragments of the *Ream Ker,* the Cambodian *Ramayana,* have been published and are on sale in Phnom Penh. The Cambodians retain an almost religious feeling about the characters in Hindu epics. In conversation, they refer to "Holy Rama" and "Holy Lakshman," his brother. In Cambodian literature today, stories about mythical kings and queens are extremely popular. They are produced as serials, each installment appearing in a separate paperback edition.

Cambodians write lyrics and sing. Naturally, Angkor provides them with a ready subject, but the Angkor of the Cambodian lyricist is different in spirit from that of the Khmers. The dreamy, nostalgic verses of Cambodian songsters today do not match our picture of ancient Angkor. They speak of sunset, of longing in the heart, and of the music of royal Angkor. One ditty refers to the kingfishers and to the singer's search for his true love. The Cambodians are romantics; the Khmers were not.

The present-day Cambodians are nimble craftsmen who have been encouraged to develop arts and crafts. The rich heritage of Khmer art stifles the production of original works, but some reinterpretation of Khmer themes is attempted—in the silverwork, for example. The Cambodian architect has just begun to combine ancient themes with a modern idiom. The results, not without merit, are said to be in the "renewed traditional" style. Copies of Khmer temples or motifs are less successful. Paintings on the walls of Buddhist monasteries or on the panels of temporary funeral pyres built for important monks display their Khmer roots with charm. Most of the monasteries themselves show a strong Thai influence. Painted masks of characters from the *Ramayana* enable the Cambodian craftsman to show his inherited skill. These links with their past are real to the Cambodians and are cultivated with care.

Theravada Buddhism is one of Cambodia's strongest links with her history—especially when one considers the impact it had on the civilization of Angkor—and it occupies an important place in present-day Cambodian life. The few Buddhist monks of Theravada whom Chou Ta-Kouan noticed at Angkor grew in numbers and influence down the centuries, but they did not rule the people as the Khmer priests had done. The Hindu religions associated with Siva and Vishnu decayed once the ideas of Theravada had undermined them. In Cambodia today, Buddhist monks may be overheard expressing horror and loathing of the Sivaite linga, but they are not really antagonistic (see Plate 54).

Although the idea of the devaraja was undermined at Angkor, the later Cambodians clung to some of the ancient beliefs about their king. Illogically, they still thought of him as a god, though this was the precise belief which Theravada Buddhism had shaken. The difference now was one of degree. While the Khmers of Angkor had an abiding faith in their god-king, those who lived after the fall of Angkor had only a superstition. Theravada Buddhism imposed its fatalism on the king and on the people. During the height of the Khmer empire, the Khmers had always felt that they could free themselves from fatalism by achievement—by the building of great temples, the digging of reservoirs, the carving of wonderful friezes. As Theravada Buddhists, they were taught that suffering was inevitable, that they and their king were trapped. Attempts to escape were doomed from the start, and the proof of their new religion lay round about them. Not only had Angkor been abandoned, but their present villages were devastated regularly by the Thai and Annamite armies as well. This was the downward spiral in which the people found themselves.

The priests, who played such an important part in the society of Angkor, have survived in modern times as a curious relic. They wear a chignon and perform ceremonial duties. The ancient Khmer corporations have disappeared. Theravada Buddhism is a classless religion, although in Ceylon caste still maintains its influence inside Buddhist communities. The two sects of Cambodian Buddhism, Mohanikay and Thommayut, are not divided according to the occupation of their members but according to status. The Thommayut is favored by the rich and by the royal family.

The Mohanikay is generally the sect of the common people. Among the other classes in Cambodian society today, the nearest equivalent to the ancient captains of militia are the head tribesmen in the hill country of northeast Cambodia. The farmers still make up the bulk of the population. The slaves have gone.

An ancient inscription of the Khmers refers to the five things deserving respect at Angkor: "riches, parentage, age, pious works, and, in fifth place, knowledge." In the Theravada Buddhist society of present-day Cambodia, the things worthy of respect are no longer the same. First, we can dismiss knowledge. The young Cambodians realize that knowledge is the key to many things, but there is nothing striking in this.

Although Cambodians easily become jealous of rich people and are pleased when they can obtain riches themselves, their religion does not teach them that riches should be respected. In this they differ from the Khmers. The average Cambodian farmer is content with a meager standard of living and does not yearn for wealth. The Chinese and the Vietnamese step in where Cambodians have renounced or let slip opportunities for making money.

As for parentage, the Cambodian peasant respects his superiors, especially members of the royal family, but in a Buddhist monastery, good or bad, high or low parentage usually counts for nothing. All monks wear the same yellow robe, and any monk who puts on airs runs the risk of breaking Buddhist precepts. While parentage was important to the Khmers, it is not of overweening importance to the Cambodians.

Despite these marked differences, the Cambodians respect age and pious works as much as the Khmers did. The elderly, especially the older Buddhist monks, command special respect; and if pious works were highly regarded at Angkor, they have attained even greater importance in Cambodia. Khmers hoped for a better reincarnation in their next life. So do the Cambodians. The Khmers hoped to achieve this end by accepting the rigid pattern which the god-kings of Angkor imposed on them. The

Cambodian hopes to achieve it through good works: by contributing money toward the ordination of a Buddhist monk, by helping to repair a tumbledown monastery, by providing food for Buddhist monks. The Cambodians perform their pious acts with much humility and considerable faith. They are not counting the price of redemption and will readily admit that their efforts may be in vain. Theravada Buddhism preaches the acceptance of suffering, and it is the Cambodians' ability to accept and forget suffering which makes them such an attractive and cheerful people. The Khmers were realists. The Cambodians are idealists.

Theravada Buddhism has provided the Cambodians, whether lay or monk, with a moral code. The Khmers did not need such a code. For them, morals were included in the rules their god-king expected them to keep. The inhabitants of Angkor were no better nor worse than their descendants, but, as Khmers, they lived in an ordered world. They were active. The Cambodians are more reflective. These are crude comparisons, but they are necessary to highlight the change which Khmer society underwent.

An ancient inscription of the Khmers refers to the seven parts of the state at Angkor: the king, his ministers, his allies, his treasure, his army, his territory, and his fortresses. The word "fortress" reminds us of Angkor Thom and Banteay Chhmar. Khmer ministers were priests, such as Hiranyadama in the reign of Jayavarman II, and Divakarapandita at the end of the eleventh century. We cannot discuss present-day Cambodian fortresses and ministers—let alone army and treasure—without entering the realm of politics. But we can examine such things as kingship, the extent of Cambodia's territory, and the meaning of ancient fortresses to her.

Instead of deposing the Cambodian king after the manner adopted by the British in Ceylon and Upper Burma, France decided to preserve the Cambodian monarchy intact. The decision reflects a difference between Great Britain and France in their attitude toward Buddhist royalty in the nineteenth century. The British, who were ruled by Queen Victoria, deposed foreign Buddhist monarchs, while the French, who were not ruled by any king or queen, protected them. In Cambodia, this was a wise decision; although the Cambodian king had to obey the French governor, an acceptable charade was played in which the king continued to command the loyalty of his own people. This was important to the Cambodians, who retained—as we have seen—a feeling that their king was a god. Cambodian peasants still regard a king as, at least, quasi-divine. To see them kneeling down in front of their king is an evocative experience. Qualities of the devaraja have survived from the days of Angkor. The title *varman* is still used. Parasols, the sign of royalty, are deployed to good effect on state occasions. Once the Cambodian people have taken a royal personage to their hearts, he may do almost anything he likes. Chou Ta-Kouan's words, written in the thirteenth century, are true of Cambodia today: ". . . these people do not fail to recognize what it is to be a king." [11]

Not only did the Khmers abandon Angkor, but their descendants, the Cambodians, lost control of the area where the ruins are situated. Now the temples have been restored to their rightful owners. Cambodia, besides being the spiritual legatee of Angkor, is also its custodian. Present-day Cambodia occupies an area much smaller than the Khmer empire of Jayavarman VII. The former Khmer territory in the Menam River valley, in the area north of the Dangrek hills, and in the Mekong River delta has been lost. The Khmer temple of Preah Vihear in the Dangrek hills was the subject of a long dispute between Cambodia and Thailand. When the case was finally heard at the International Court at the Hague in 1962, Cambodia won.[12] A big change affecting Cambodia's territory was the opening of her first seaport at Kompong Som (renamed Sihanoukville). Apart from one or two small fishing ports, this was the first harbor of consequence to be built on a coast which once supported the great emporia of Funan.

The ruins of Angkor, particularly those of Angkor Wat,

11 Chou Ta-Kouan, p. 35.

12 *Case Concerning the Temple of Preah Vihear* (Cambodia v. Thailand), Merits, Judgment of 15 June 1962. International Court of Justice Reports, The Hague, 1962, pp. 6–146.

have become a symbol for the Cambodian people. Their national flag carries a representation of Angkor Wat, and every foreign visitor is shown the ruins by his Cambodian host. For most Cambodians, Angkor is a place of pilgrimage, especially at the Cambodian New Year. Even in villages far distant from the Khmer capital, there is a pious feeling that to pass one's life without going at least once to Angkor is wrong. Nowadays, most ancient Khmer temples are regarded as places of pilgrimage for Buddhists, regardless of their original religious affiliation. Underneath their Buddhist beliefs, the Cambodians also worship a number of nature spirits, called *neak ta,* and these are sometimes housed in ruined Khmer temples. It is even possible that some Sivaite or Vishnuite customs still linger on disguised as worship of *neak ta.* Carved earth pillars resembling lingas are found in some Cambodian villages today, and their presence is another indication of ancient beliefs underlying Theravada Buddhism.

We have written of Khmers and Cambodians. In their own language, the Cambodians refer to themselves as "Khmer," for Khmers and Cambodians are one and the same. The distinction between Khmer and Cambodian is made simply for convenience, to avoid the continual use of "ancient" and "modern." The temples of the former are the natural priceless heritage of the latter, and they know their worth. The bas-relief galleries of Angkor Wat are eleven times as long as the Bayeux tapestry and five times the length of the Parthenon frieze. Angkor Thom is more than eight times as large as the Roman town of Timgad in Numidia. The temple area of Preah Khan (Angkor) is almost twice the size of the Mayan city of Copan in Honduras. True, we should guard against using too many superlatives about Khmer ruins. Neither Angkor Wat nor the Bayon nor Ta Keo rises to half the height of the First Pyramid at Giza. To build the dome of Santa Sophia in Constantinople or the former spire of Malmesbury Abbey in England required techniques which were unknown to the Khmers. Yet the Khmers excelled in using their own well-tried elements—the recessed pyramid, the tower, the gallery, and the lotus decoration.

Perhaps the greatest single heritage of the modern Khmers is one which belongs to the people of the world —the joy of knowing a "lost city" through tangible remains, of not being confined to dusty tomes which only describe an irretrievable past. Few ancient civilizations have emerged from obscurity to boast of so much present beauty or to reveal their way of life so abundantly.

# *Glossary*

| | |
|---|---|
| ANGKOR PERIOD | The period of Khmer history from A.D. 802 to 1432 |
| ANNAM | Former name for central Vietnam |
| ANNAMITES | Former name for the Vietnamese |
| APSARAS | Celestial dancer (female), said to conduct fallen warriors to their rest |
| AVATAR | Incarnation of a Hindu deity |
| BANTEAY | Cambodian word for "citadel" |
| BAS-RELIEF | Carving or sculpture that projects slightly from the background on which it is carved |
| BENG | Cambodian word for "pool" |
| BODHISATTVA | A future Buddha |
| CAMBODIAN | Synonymous with Khmer, but used in this book for the present inhabitants of Cambodia |
| CHAM | An inhabitant of the ancient kingdom of Champa; also its ancient language |
| CHEN-LA | Ancient Chinese name for Cambodia |
| DAI-VIET | Ancient name for Annam |
| DEVARAJA | Sanskrit designation meaning "god-king" |
| DHARMA | Sanskrit word meaning "doctrine" |
| DVARAPALA | Guardian deity |
| EFEO | Abbreviated form of *École Française d'Extrême-Orient* (French School of the Far East) |
| FUNAN | The first historical kingdom of south Indochina |
| GARUDA | Mythical bird—the mount of Vishnu |
| GOPURA | Sanskrit term used for entrances to Khmer temples |
| HARIHARA | A Hindu deity combining Hari (Vishnu) and Hara (Siva) |
| INDOCHINA | A term first used by the eighteenth-century Danish geographer Malte-Brun to |

205

designate the peninsula where peoples influenced by India (e.g., the Khmers) and by China (e.g., the Vietnamese) lived

JATAKAS Buddhist stories

JAYA Sanskrit word for "victory"

KEV (or KEO) Cambodian word for "jewel"

KHMER Synonymous with Cambodian, but used in this book for the ancient inhabitants of Angkor

KOMPONG Cambodian word for "port"—either by the sea or on a riverbank

LINGA Phallic emblem of Siva—made of stone or glass or metal. The anglicized form of this word is *lingam*, but it is customary for people writing in English about Angkor to use *linga*, since it looks and sounds more pleasing than *lingam*

LOKESVARA A bodhisattva—Lord of the World

MAHAYANA Northern school of Buddhism

MANDARA A mountain from Hindu mythology which forms the churn in the churning of the Sea of Milk legend

MERU Mountain from Hindu mythology, said to be at the center of the universe, and represented by the Khmers in their pyramidal temple-mountains—e.g., the Phnom Bakheng

MON Inhabitant of ancient kingdom in the Menam River valley; also a language

MON-KHMER Name for an ethnic group stretching from Burma to the China Sea; includes Khmers and Mons

NAGA Mythical serpent

NAGARA Sanskrit word for "city," from which "Angkor" is derived

NEAK TA Cambodian designation for nature spirits

O Cambodian word for "stream"

PANDITA Sanskrit word for "high priest"

PHNOM Cambodian word for "hill"

PLAINE DES JONCS French name ("plain of the junks") for a locality in south Indochina

PRASAT Ancient tower containing sanctuary

PRE–ANGKOR PERIOD The period of Khmer history from the decline of Funan (sixth century A.D.) until A.D. 802

| | |
|---|---|
| PREAH | Cambodian word for "holy" |
| PREI | Cambodian word for "forest" |
| PURA | Sanskrit word for "town" |
| SAMRÉ | Name of a tribe living near Angkor |
| SANSKRIT | The sacred language of ancient India |
| SINICIZED | Influenced by China (cf. anglicized) |
| SPEAN | Cambodian word for "bridge" |
| SRA | Cambodian word for "sacred pool" |
| STUNG | Cambodian word for "river" |
| STUPA | Buddhist monument |
| SVAY | Cambodian word for "mango" |
| TANTRIC | A recently coined adjective used when referring to the Buddhist writings of Nepal and Tibet |
| TATAKA | Sanskrit word for "pond" |
| THAI | Inhabitant of an ancient (and modern) kingdom in the Menam River valley and environs; also the language. Same as "Siamese" |
| THERAVADA | Southern school of Buddhism |
| THOM | Cambodian word for "big" |
| TONLE SAP | Cambodian expression used when referring to the Great Lake |
| VARMAN | Sanskrit word literally meaning "protected" but having acquired the meaning of "protector" |
| VEDAS | Traditional written sources of Hindu religions |
| VIHEAR | Cambodian word for "sanctuary" |
| WAT (or VAT) | Buddhist monastery |

# A Selected Bibliography

A complete bibliography of Khmer studies would be too lengthy to include here. The following list, which touches on kindred subjects as well as on Angkor itself, is intended to help the general reader and those interested in doing further research.

Asia House Gallery, *Khmer Sculpture.* New York, 1961. Well-presented photographs of Khmer sculpture in United States museums and private collections. The volume includes a Preface by George Montgomery and a critical essay by Ad Reinhardt.

Aymonier, Etienne, *Le Cambodge.* Paris, 1900–3. This three-volume work is still useful. An index by G. Coedès was published separately in 1911 (Paris).

Barth, Auguste, and Bergaigne, Abel, *Inscriptions Sanscrites du Cambodge.* Paris, 1885. The inscriptions of Cambodia are scattered in various publications. This volume and Coedès' *Inscriptions du Cambodge* have to be supplemented by searching through the *Journal Asiatique* (Paris) and the *Bulletin de l'École Française d'Extrême-Orient* (Hanoi-Saigon-Paris).

Bhattacharya, Kamaleswar, *Les Religions Brahmaniques dans l'ancien Cambodge d'après l'épigraphie et l'iconographie.* Paris, 1961.

Boisselier, Jean, *Le Cambodge.* Paris, 1966.

———, *Tendances de l'art Khmer.* Paris, 1956. A commentary on twenty-four Khmer masterpieces from the National Museum, Phnom Penh. A good book for the general reader and for visitors to Cambodia.

Bosch, F. D. K., *The Golden Germ: an Introduction to Indian Symbolism.* The Hague, 1960.

———, "Le temple d'Angkor Wat," *Bulletin de l'École Française d'Extrême-Orient,* XXXII (Hanoi, Vietnam, 1932), 7–21.

Boxer, C. R., ed., *South China in the Sixteenth Century.* London, 1953. Contains a translation of the *Tractado* (1569) of Gaspar da Cruz based on the pioneer translation of Samuel Purchas (1625). The passages on Cambodia have informative footnotes, including some by Judith Jacob (née Stead), the author of several important articles on Khmer linguistics.

Briggs, Lawrence Palmer, *The Ancient Khmer Empire.* Philadelphia, 1955. An essential book, with an extensive Bibliography. Although it contains some mistakes, it brings together in unique fashion the findings of many scholars.

Buddhist Institute, *Cérémonies des douze mois.* Phnom Penh, Cambodia, n.d.

———, *Cérémonies privées des Cambodgiens.* Phnom Penh, Cambodia, 1958. These two publications of the Buddhist Institute are useful introductions to Cambodian life.

*Case Concerning the Temple of Preah Vihear* (Cambodia v. Thailand), Merits, Judgment of 15 June 1962. International Court of Justice Reports, The Hague, 1962, pp. 6–146. A fascinating document.

Chau Ju-Qua, *Records of Foreign Nations,* trans. by Friedrich Hirth and W. W. Rockhill. St. Petersburg, Russia, 1911.

Chou Ta-Kouan, *Mémoires sur les coutumes du Cambodge de Tcheou Ta-Kouan,* trans. by Paul Pelliot. Paris, 1951. A revised version of Pelliot's 1902 translation, but with incomplete commentary.

Christie, Anthony, "The Sea-Locked Lands: the Diverse Traditions of South-East Asia," Chapter Ten of *The Dawn of Civilisation.* London, 1961.

Clifford, Sir Hugh, *The Downfall of the Gods.* London, 1911. A novel.

Coedès, George, *Angkor.* Hong Kong, 1963. This book is a translation of essays originally published under the title *Pour mieux comprendre Angkor.*

———, *Bronzes Khmers.* Ars Asiatica, No. 5. Paris, 1923.

———, "La destination funéraire des grands monuments Khmèrs." *Bulletin de l'École Française d'Extrême-Orient,* XL (Hanoi, Vietnam, 1940), 315–343.

———, *Les États Hindouisés d'Indochine et d'Indonésie,* rev. ed. Paris, 1964.

———, ed., *Inscriptions du Cambodge,* 8 vols. Hanoi, Vietnam, and Paris, 1937–66.

———, *Les Peuples de la péninsule Indochinoise.* Paris, 1962. A bibliography of Coedès' work was published in *Artibus Asaie,* Vol. XXIV, Nos. 3–4 (Ascona, Switzerland, 1961).

———, "Le serment des fonctionnaires de Suryavarman I."

*Bulletin de l'École Française d'Extrême-Orient,* XIII (Hanoi, Vietnam, 1913), 11–17.

Coomaraswamy, A., *The Transformation of Nature in Art.* New York, 1956. A reissue of classic essays on the theory of art in India, China, and Europe.

Coral-Remusat, Gilberte de, *L'Art Khmer: les grandes étapes de son évolution.* Paris, 1951.

Dannaud, J-P., *Cambodge.* Saigon, Vietnam, 1956. Excellent photographs of the Cambodian scene.

Dasgupta, Surendranath, *Southern Schools of Saivism,* Vol. 5, *A History of Indian Philosophy.* Cambridge, Eng., 1955.

De Berval, René, ed., *Présence du Cambodge.* Saigon, Vietnam, 1955. This special number of the periodical *France-Asie* (Tokyo), makes a worthwhile introduction to Cambodia and the Khmers. It includes essays by a wide range of contributors, among them, G. Coedès.

Delaporte, Louis, *Voyage au Cambodge.* Paris, 1880.

Delvert, Jean, *Le Paysan Cambodgien.* Paris, 1961.

Dufour, Henri, and Carpeaux, Charles, *Le Bayon d'Angkor Thom.* Paris, 1910. Sixteen folios of plates showing the Bayon bas-reliefs.

Dupont, Pierre, *L'Archéologie mône de Dvaravati.* Paris, 1959.

————, *La Statuaire préangkorienne.* Ascona, Switzerland, 1955.

Filliozat, Jean, "Les Divisions sociales de l'Inde," Preface to G. Olivier, *Anthropologie des tamouls du sud de l'Inde.* Paris, 1961.

Finot, Louis, "L'Archéologie Indochinoise: 1917–1930." *Bulletin de la Commission Archéologique Indochinoise* (Paris, 1930), 1–100.

————, *Le Bouddhisme.* Phnom Penh, Cambodia, 1957.

————, "Inscriptions d'Angkor." *Bulletin de l'École Française d'Extrême-Orient,* XXV (Hanoi, Vietnam, 1925), 289–407.

————, "L'inscription de Ban Theat." *Bulletin de l'École Française d'Extrême-Orient,* XII (Hanoi, Vietnam, 1912), 1–28.

————, et al., eds., *Le Temple d'Angkor Vat.* Paris, 1927–32. Seven volumes of plates covering the architecture, ornamental sculpture, and bas-reliefs of Angkor Wat.

Foucher, A., *L'Art Gréco-Bouddhique du Gandhara.* Paris, 1905–18.

Ghosh, Manomohan, *A History of Cambodia.* Saigon, Vietnam, 1960. An important but uneven book which attacks many accepted ideas about Angkor.

Giteau, Madeleine, *Khmer Sculpture and the Angkor Civilization.* London, 1965.

Glaize, Maurice, *Les Monuments du groupe d'Angkor.* Saigon, Vietnam, 1958. A guidebook.

Goloubew, Victor, "Le Cheval Balaha." *Bulletin de l'École Française d'Extrême-Orient,* XXVII (Hanoi, Vietnam, 1927), 223–38.

Gourou, Pierre, *La Terre et l'homme en extrême-orient.* Paris, 1940.

Groslier, Bernard-Philippe, *Angkor: Art and Civilisation.* (Revised Edition) London, 1966.

——, *Angkor et le Cambodge au XVIᵉ siècle d'après les sources Portugaises et Espagnoles.* Paris, 1958. Although this book deals with the sixteenth century, it contains much material pertinent to the Angkor period of Khmer history. M. Groslier has, through his writings and conversation, made me aware of much—for which I am indeed grateful.

Groslier, Georges, *À l'Ombre d'Angkor.* Paris, 1916. An evocative description of journeys to Preah Vihear, Ta Prohm, Beng Mealea, Banteay Chhmar, and other points.

——, *Les Collections Khmères de Musée Albert Sarraut à Phnom Penh.* Ars Asiatica, No. 16. Paris, 1931. Can be read in conjunction with G. Coedès' essay on Khmer bronzes.

——, *Recherches sur les Cambodgiens.* Paris, 1921. An important book, especially for understanding life at Angkor.

Hallade, Madeleine, *Arts de l'Asie ancienne—thèmes et motifs,* Vol. 2, *L'Asie du sud-est.* Paris, 1954. An introduction to the ancient art of Ceylon, Java, Cambodia, Champa, and other regions. The volume contains 384 drawings and a chronological table.

Jouveau-Dubreuil, G., *Iconography of Southern India,* trans. by A. C. Martin. Paris, 1937.

Kramrisch, Stella, *The Art of India.* London, 1954.

Krom, N. J., *Barabudur.* The Hague, 1927. A two-volume description of the great temple-mountain in Java.

Lajonquière, Lunet de, *Inventaire descriptif des monuments du Cambodge.* Paris, 1902–11.

Lamb, Alastair, "Chandi Bukit Batu Pahat." *Federation Museums Journal,* V (Kuala Lumpur, Malaysia, 1960).

——, "Early Hindu and Buddhist Settlement in Northern Malaya and Southern Thailand." *Federation Museums Journal,* VI (Kuala Lumpur, Malaysia, 1961).

Leclère, Adhemard, *Le Bouddhisme au Cambodge.* Paris, 1899.

——, *La Crémation et les rites funéraires au Cambodge.* Hanoi, Vietnam, 1907.

Le May, Reginald, "Ornamental Khmer Bronzes," *The Bur-*

*lington Magazine,* Vol. LXXIX, No. 63 (London, 1941), 111–13.

Levy, Paul, *Buddhism: A Mystery Religion?* London, 1957.

Loti, Pierre, *Un Pèlerin d'Angkor.* Paris, 1912.

Luce, G. H., "Note on the Peoples of Burma in the 12th–13th Century." *Journal of the Burma Research Society,* Vol. XLII, No. 1 (Rangoon, June, 1959), 52–74.

———, and Pe Maung Tin, *The Glass Palace Chronicle of the Kings of Burma.* London, 1923.

Macdonald, Malcolm, *Angkor.* London, 1958. An entertaining and lighthearted book about Angkor and the Cambodian scene. It contains more than eighty pleasing photographs of Khmer temples, statues, and reliefs by Loke Wan Tho.

Majumdar, R. C., *Kambuja-Desa.* Madras, India, 1944.

Malleret, Louis, *L'Archéologie du delta du Mekong.* Paris, 1959–62. Description of the excavations at Oc-Eo; important for the study of Funan.

Malraux, André, *The Royal Way,* trans. by Stuart Gilbert. London, 1935. A novel.

Marchal, Henri, *L'Architecture comparée dans l'Inde et l'extrême orient.* Paris, 1944.

Marchal, Sappho, *Costumes et parures Khmères d'après les dévatas d'Angkor Vat.* Paris, 1927.

Martini, François, "En Marge du Ramayana Cambodgien." *Bulletin de l'École Française d'Extrême-Orient,* XXXVIII (Hanoi, Vietnam, 1938), 285–95.

———, "En Marge du Ramayana Cambodgien." *Journal Asiatique,* Vol. CLXXXVIII, No. 1 (Paris, 1950), 81–90.

———, and Bernard, Solange, *Contes populaires inédits du Cambodge.* Paris, 1946.

Maspero, Georges, *Le Royaume du Champa.* Paris, 1928.

Maspero, Henri, "La Frontière de l'Annam et du Cambodge du VIII au XIVe siècles." *Bulletin de l'École Française d'Extrême-Orient.* XVIII (Hanoi, Vietnam, 1918), 29–36.

Ma Touan-Lin, *Ethnographie des peuples étrangers,* trans. by d'Hervey de Saint Denys. Paris, 1883.

Mauger, Henri, "Preah Khan de Kompong Svay." *Bulletin de l'École Française d'Extrême-Orient,* XXXIX (Hanoi, Vietnam, 1939), 197–220.

Monod, G-H., *Le Cambodgien.* Paris, 1931.

Moule, A. C., and Pelliot, Paul, *Marco Polo: the Description of the World.* London, 1938.

Mus, Paul, "Le Sourire d'Angkor." *Artibus Asiae,* Vol. XXIV, Nos. 3–4 (Ascona, Switzerland, 1961), 363–81.

Olivier, Georges, *Les Populations du Cambodge.* Paris, 1956.

Pannetier, A., "Sentences et proverbs cambodgiens." *Bulletin de l'École Française d'Extrême-Orient*, XV (Hanoi, Vietnam, 1915), 47–71.

Parmentier, Henri, *L'Art Khmèr classique*. Paris, 1939.

————, "Les Bas-reliefs de Banteay Chhmar." *Bulletin de l'École Française d'Extrême-Orient*, X (Hanoi, Vietnam, 1910), 205–22. Owing to its remote location, Banteay Chhmar has received less attention than the Bayon or Angkor Wat. The bas-reliefs (see Plate 31) were photographed under the direction of General de Beylié but were not published.

————, et al., *Le Temple d'Icvarapura*. Paris, 1926. Plates of Banteay Srei. The text is now outdated.

Pelliot, Paul, "Deux itinéraires de Chine en Inde à la fin du VIIIᵉ siècle." *Bulletin de l'École Française d'Extrême-Orient*, IV (Hanoi, Vietnam, 1904), 131–385.

————, "Fou-Nan." *Bulletin de l'École Française d'Extrême-Orient*, III (Hanoi, Vietnam, 1903), 248–303.

Porée, Guy, and Maspero, Eveline, *Moeurs et coutumes des Khmers*. Paris, 1938. A valuable introduction to the Cambodian mind.

Porée-Maspero, Eveline, *Étude sur les rites agraires des Cambodgiens*. Paris, 1962–64.

Przyluski, Jean, "Is Angkor-Wat a temple or a tomb?" *Journal of the Indian Society of Oriental Art*, V (Calcutta, 1937), 131–144.

Pym, Christopher, ed., *Henri Mouhot's Diary*. New York, 1967. The diary of Henri Mouhot, who rediscovered Angkor for the Western world.

————, *The Road to Angkor*. London, 1959. Describes a journey from the ancient capital of Champa to Angkor.

Quaritch Wales, H. G., *Angkor and Rome*. London, 1965.

Ray, Niharranjan, *Theravada Buddhism in Burma*. Calcutta, 1946.

Rowland, Benjamin, *The Art and Architecture of India*, Baltimore, 1953. The final section of this book (Part Six) covers the art of Ceylon, Cambodia, Thailand, Burma, and Java.

Sarkar, Kalyan Kumar, "Mahayana Buddhism in Fu-Nan." *Sino-Indian Studies*, Vol. V, No. 1 (Santiniketan, India, 1955), 69ff.

Saurin, Edmond, "Quelques remarques sur les grès d'Angkor." *Bulletin de l'École Française d'Extrême-Orient*, XLVI (Paris, 1954), 619–34.

Seidenfaden, Eric, "Complement à l'inventaire descriptif des monuments du Cambodge pour les quatre provinces du Siam oriental." *Bulletin de l'École Française d'Extrême-Orient,* XXII (Hanoi, Vietnam, 1922), 55–99.

Sitwell, Osbert, *Escape with Me.* London, 1939. A travel book about Angkor and Peking.

Souyris-Roland, A., "La poterie dans le Sud-Cambodge." *Bulletin de la Societé des Études Indochinoises,* XXV, No. 3 (Saigon, Vietnam, 1950), 307–311.

Steinberg, David J., ed., *Cambodia: Its People, Its Society, Its Culture.* New Haven, Conn., 1957.

Stern, Philipe, *Les Monuments Khmers du style du Bayon et Jayavarman VII.* Paris, 1965.

Stutterheim, W. F., *Studies in Indonesian Archaeology.* The Hague, 1956. A translation of earlier studies.

Thiounn, Samdach Chaufea Veang, *Les danses Cambodgiennes.* Hanoi, Vietnam, 1930.

Thomson, J., *The Antiquities of Cambodia.* Edinburgh, 1867. "Mr. Thomson the photographer gentleman," as the Thai king called him, took some of the best early photographs of Angkor.

Toynbee, Arnold, *East to West.* London, 1958.

Trouvé, G. M., "Travaux de sondages executés sous le dallage du sanctuaire central d'Angkor Vat." *Bulletin de l'École Française d'Extrême-Orient,* XXXV (Hanoi, Vietnam, 1935), 483–86. Trouvé's brilliant career at Angkor was cut short in a tragic manner. He had a genius for finding things —as was appropriate in a man of his name and calling.

Wheeler, Sir Robert Eric Mortimer, *Rome Beyond the Imperial Frontiers.* London, 1955.

Wolters, O. W., "Chen-li-fu." *The Journal of the Siam Society,* XLVIII (Bangkok, 1960), 1–35.

———, "Tambralinga." *Bulletin of the School of Oriental and African Studies,* Vol. XXI, No. 3 (London, 1958), 587–607. Important contributions to the study of Jayavarman VII's empire.

# INDEX

# INDEX

Ancient ruins of the Angkor civilization are shown in italics.

217